Sometimes I Lie Awake at Night

Seylah Love

Published by Seylah Love, 2024.

SOMETIMES I LIE AWAKE AT NIGHT

First edition. September 23, 2024.

ISBN: 979-8227508195

Written by Seylah Love.

Table of Contents

SOMETIMES I LIE AWAKE AT NIGHT

The Cosmic Musings of a Magnolia Flower

By Seylah Love

Prologue

Eulogies and Symphonies

Tears stream down my face as the currents within my soul pull, push- wade and thrash.

Wondering if this tear stained face will ever come to see and feel the solace and joy of a sunny days glory again.

I traverse the depths of death and despair. Loss and betrayal. Revelations and the masochistic pleasure of Truth's fierce execution and judgement.

Coming into the light Hidden trespasses revealed,

The origins of the ghastly hauntings and missing pieces that always scratched at the back of my heart and spirit.

I draw out my courage as fear draws out its claws.

I feel so deeply into it,

body, mind and All.

It falls entranced by my stare and my pythonizing song.

It kneels awestricken,

overcome with defeat and the burning desire to now serve.

They question how I've become so unmoved by their screeching sirens and pitiless attacks.

Wondering how come they can no longer trap me into a mess of violent self destruction and spiritual desolation.

Grief and fear become my unbeseeming companions.

Together we dance to the rhythms of the night,

in the chambers of my heart that have been reserved for us and no one else.

I sway and listen as I stitch together the pieces of my soul in need of salvation and mending.

Together We sit under the moons glowing body,

Singing, wailing, laughing and howling. Again and again. Over and over.

Until the pain turns into peace, power, and medicine.

Until the tears turn into laughter, madness and consolation.

Ready for release and transmutation.

Ready for release and transformation.

It seems now only death, grief and fear understand me well.

My unforeseen, newly made best-friends from the depths of the shadow realms.

I ask,

Have I gone too far out?

Or have I simply arrived at the shore of the kingdom of heaven more wholly than before?

The sound of my screams echo and ripple across the seas.

It seems the shadows are the only things that hold the peace of which Im deeply in need.

The fire that burns deep within,

brings the hope, balance and energy needed—

to stay focused on the Holy Spirits presence and commandments.

The loss of a father.

The loss of an opportunity.

The loss of a reality.

The loss of a self.

The loss of a mind.

The loss of a spirit.

The loss. The loss. The blow of it all.

One after another, like a suffocating fog.

In one fell swoop the destruction rained like a waterfall.

I worked overtime to become the eye of the storm,

Me, myself and I alone.

Terrified but courageous nonetheless.

My soul fortified in Gods presence.

I bend every which way but never break,

as i confide in the warmness of deaths embrace.

I find peace in my growing understanding and acceptance of its wisdom and purpose.

Confiding in the lord as i thrash about in the primordial waters of the sacred void of which I was birthed.

Gestating. Growing.

A new heart, a new conscious,

A new story.

Tears stream down my face as my heart screams, wails, and shivers.

Until my fingertips are drenched in blood,

A memorialization of my efforts.

Until the tears turn into holy water—inviting my baptism and initiation.

Full circle —the new world is ready and the void unfurls.

The ouroboros eats and then out comes her new form.

As she rises white as snow,

Having made it through the trenches of the deepest parts of the underworld.

Hand in hand with her spiritual supports, known and loved.

They pass around the rum and yell "Seylah is the One".

They dance in praise as they pour blessings upon the crown of which they have ordained.

Over who I was always destined to be and embody in the name of our liberation, legacy and empowerment.

Over the graves of our loved ones and the one that cradled my soul,

as I transformed in the belly of Gaias temple.

They watched intensely as I learned to dig and rise myself from six feet under.

Body submerged in the consecrated southern soil that holds the remnants of my ancestors memories and blood.

I rose from the depths unto earths surface and was kissed so gently and tenderly by the heavens.

I learned that death is truly never the end but the brightest beginning,

as I spit and cough out the soil that healed and nourished me beyond my skin, deep into my organs.

I rise with the rising sun and give offerings of gratitude and appreciation to it and the universe.

To God, my ancestors and universal supports.

I am greeted by smiling faces full of pride,

Deeply embraced in celebratory howls, laughter and applause.

Congratulating me and celebrating us for all our of progress and achievements reached.

Together as one in the name of the Almighty.

I turn to see the face of my newly arrived ancestor.

Oh How i thank you dearly for the ways you have already show up for me in spirit.

25 years we were robbed of life,

But through death I realized we've been gifted an eternity of unity and togetherness.

Death and grief becomes a place of reformation, purification and restoration for me.

No longer foes but strong and powerful teachers and friends.

A brush with Death, which brought me heart to heart with my purest and truest self.

An intertwining and emergence.

No longer fearful or in Denial of my dreams, destiny and purpose.

I laid in the hospital bed and let deep gratitude pour out of me.

Praising his name and crying at the showings of his glory and mercy.

Fearing him with a humble and sincere heart, divine I thank thee.

Renewing our covenant.

Vowing myself to our sacred union and mergence in ways I was once unable or too hesitant.

I've given of myself completely with no inhibitions or worries.

Committing my life fully to this higher purpose and calling.

A sequence of events ushered in by the spirit of death,

Have helped me truly know and intertwine with the holy mother and father of my creation.

Through this transformation Ive unlocked and resurrected,

pieces of myself and our birthrights that had been locked away, lost and stolen.

She's the butterfly effect striving to leave generational impact.

My God she has risen.

Sprouted and blossomed From the ashes and soil of fire and brimstone.

Not of hell, but of the most trying thing in this world.

The ebb and flow of the human condition,

our existence.

She is sovereign within her being.

Free within her mind, body and spirit.

A being once shy, timid and easily disturbed,

Has now become The thing of sacred testament,

To blest power, strength, confidence and courage.

Whose story has only truly just begun and comes forth from the springs of the all eternal.

Immortalized Tears stream down my face as the currents within my soul pull, push and wade.

And I look to the heavens with a smile on my face,

And a godly, golden-flaming, bleeding heart in my chest.

Wrapped in the Holy sacraments and texts.

My beloved Seylah.

You rise. You rise. You rise in excellence.

In the name of the Holy Mother, Father and Sacred Child.

Together at last.

SOMETIMES I LIE AWAKE AT NIGHT

— Seylah S. Love

The Pain of Loving You.

Heartbreak and heartache.
It comes so fast and sudden as the waves of emotions leave you gasping for air.
You can feel the pain creeping through your veins,
Slowly engulfing every crevice and every fiber of your being.
Making it feel like you're made of nothing at all.
Weightless— until the growing ache in your chest makes you feel dense like stone.
Inhaling feels like 9-5 work.
The warmth leaves your body as the world around you collapses and swallows you into darkness.
Every beat of your heart feels like a betrayal to your body.
You can feel the cold rippling through every limb and every muscle.
Even your bones begin to feel like at any moment they will crumble.
For a moment at its peak, you get high off of the hurt.
Then the high passes leaving you numb and dumbstruck.
Wishing for anything in that moment to stop the growing hole in your heart.
Searching for anything to shut it off, no matter the cost.
Physically feeling love die is torturous.
Physically feeling love die is hell at its finest.

Audacious Mf.

How dare you do that to me?
How dare you come into my life and make me fall head over heels in
love with you like this?
The nerve of you to ever walk your way into my heart and make a
place.
How dare you open my heart to this kind of immense passion are you
insane?
Who the fuck do you think you are leaving me heartbroken like this?
Loving me the way you did and then leaving so suddenly.
You lied to me.
You promised it was me and you from beginning to end.
I'm so angry at myself how could I ever let you bring me here?
Sitting in these feelings,
Wishing I could go back and make better decisions.
I'm so angry at myself, how dare I still love you?
You broke my fucking heart and I still fucking love you.
What a scam this love thing is to be quite fucking honest.

Pyromaniac.

Why start a fire just to watch it burn?
You sat smugly as it moved like a tornado through our home.
The flames consumed me bit by bit as I begged for your remorse.
And you watched with no concern as our love grew twisted and
scorched.
Why start a fire just to watch it burn?
You left my heart in ashes and you sat with no remorse.
You gave me one last glance and then you said to me,
"Maybe one day in the future we can do this thing again."
You turned around and walked away full and in one piece.
As I sat in the ruins desolate and broken.
It was on that day I vowed to never love again,
And I cursed the day I ever placed my heart into your hands.

Raw.

Sex is a funny thing.
I wish I would have understood what I was getting myself into with
you.
You penetrated my mind, body, and soul on more levels than you
could ever know.
Your body, your kisses, and your touches were my favorite drug.
You made me feel higher than any strain of weed could.
I craved you so much, you were so sweet to me.
I could eat you for hours, for days on repeat.
You loved to see me orgasmed out, weak in the knees.
You loved to relish in your work and I loved to see you pleased.
Drunk in love, you'd leave a trail of sweet kisses over me.
The puddles I would leave were your favorite thing to see.
The loud whispers of my own heart begging for mercy.
Every time it got warm though, is when it seemed you'd go to leave.
Our love on your sheets would fade,
As the memories we made silenced and packed away.
You'd take the last ounce of love I had and store it away.
My fire starter, my fire baby they never warned me in any way.
I never saw you coming but how painful it has been to watch you walk
away.

I Knew Better.

Why is it that when we know better we don't always do better?
Especially when you throw romance into the matter.
My heart thought she knew it all but she forgot to bring logic into
question.
Temptation and desire made me blind to the reality of what was
happening.
My need for love and affection became the eye of my destruction.
And the harder I fell, the harsher I would feel your absence.
And the more unreal this death would feel—no this can't be
happening.
I knew better. I knew better. But if only I could,
Go back in time and do better how I should've.
When it was all said and done you were the first one to go.
In the ruins of the mess we created here lies the tombstone,
Of a glorious love turned sour, turned poison to our bones.
Now it's just me, my thoughts, and the ruins of what was.
I knew better, I knew better, how could I not have known?
That this love wasn't the one and you were only looking for
somewhere warm.

A Magnolias Interlude #1:

To Honor Thyself is to Love Thyself

Sometimes the best decisions that we can make for ourselves are the ones that challenge our comfortability. Sometimes change will not occur until we recognize that the sword in our hand isn't just for show but for real-life action. Sometimes the Divine will wait on us to get sick of our own shit so that we will finally sit still and take head. A hard head will make for a soft ass and sometimes that fall is what's needed for us to finally disillusion ourselves of the bullshit and do what needs to be done for our healing, growth, and progression. Sometimes the answer and the way out is in the truth we are unwilling to see, sit with, and accept. Sometimes we question God when we need to be questioning ourselves. Sometimes the reason we feel like we are stuck and cannot move forward is that we refuse to be honest about the ways that we are resisting what needs to be done, embraced, released, understood, accepted, etc. and in doing so we wind up consciously or unconsciously betraying and sabotaging ourselves because of our lack of self-responsibility, accountability, and awareness. Sometimes we choose to sit in the illusions and comfort zones because we are scared of the unknown. Because we feel intimidated by the work and the many responsibilities that we know will be waiting for us once the distractions are gone and playtime is over. Sometimes we choose ignorance and blindness for the temporary bliss and mental relief it provides even if it stunts our growth and progression for a while. Sometimes we will settle for mediocrity and less than what we know we deserve because we are afraid of being alone with ourselves and in doing these things we are actively choosing to dishonor, disrespect, oppress, and delay ourselves. The thing about the truth is that it will empower you and set you free. It will help push you onto a path that supports and sustains you rather than stunt and slowly break you down. The thing about clarity is that it will bring you closer to things that are real, tried, and true, but we have to be willing to be temporarily uncomfortable as we do the work to fully purge and clean out everything that isn't. The thing about self-responsibility, accountability, and awareness is that it will challenge you and demand you stand on business, but in turn, it will amplify the joy, peace, harmony, stability, and security you grow and sustain inside and out. These personal tools will help you become more authentic, refined, and self-actualized as a whole. They will encourage you to love and appreciate who and where you are in the now, while lovingly guiding you towards who you wish to become and where you wish to be. They will help usher you into personal excellence, expansion, and maturity by demanding that you do better because now you know better. When we choose to see past our own bullshit and wield our sword of truth with determination, courage, and focus, at that moment we are honoring, loving, and caring for ourselves deeply and intimately. We begin to see and love ourselves the way the Universe and the Divine do. When we say no to self-betrayal, self-neglect, self-sabotage, and abandonment, we are saying yes to self-love, self-respect, and self-care and empowerment.

If anything is worth fighting for it is the fulfillment of our spiritual and physical potential and purpose. The only way we can achieve this is by choosing to honor ourselves every day and by staying committed to our path through thick and thin. We must utilize our personal power and free will wisely and responsibly, as we muster up the courage and confidence to make the appropriate choices and decisions that honor the promises and commitments that we have made to our hearts and souls. We must follow through with might as we listen to and adhere to the guidance of our hearts, even if it calls for us to make choices and take actions that require we put ourselves first and other people's wants, needs, and expectations last. Sometimes that looks like letting go with grace and appreciation when something has run its course. In this we are choosing to make meaningful external sacrifices so that we are not unnecessarily internally sacrificing ourselves. Sometimes honoring ourselves looks like willingly entering seasons of hermit mode so that we can do the necessary inner- work required before we can reap our blessings and/or enter the next chapter within our wheel of destiny. Sometimes it looks like challenging our comfortability and learning to find steadiness in the temporary discomfort. Sometimes it looks like holding our own hands as we dare to shatter and break through the limiting stories, conditionings and confining illusions that influence us through open, honest, and shame-free self-reflection and introspection. It looks like being brutally honest about what we need to grow, be full, and be happy, and pursuing that fiercely and unapologetically. It looks like holding on to that vision and not being afraid to do what needs to be done virtuously to make it happen. Even if we have to do it trembling a little, the courage that we are exuding and faith we are embodying will carry us through and forward. We just have to be willing to take that leap of, follow our inner compass and trust in the Divine and our abilities. We just have to give it the best that we have. Sometimes it's saying no and go to hell in that order. Honoring ourselves means living for ourselves. Loving each version of ourselves as we grow and learn. Honoring ourselves is deeply caring for ourselves beyond skincare routines and aesthetics. It's getting up every day and choosing Self, choosing Truth, choosing Love, and taking conscious actions that support the free, liberated, and empowered tone we set over our souls and our lives. It isn't always easy to honor and be deeply engaged with self and all that is, but it is possible and it is how we live a life not wasted and of our design. It's how we fulfill our souls beyond just physical materials and matters. It's how we ensure joy, meaning and purpose fill our life, making it a life worth living. It's how we ensure we will become the powerful sovereign beings we were all born to be.

After the Storm.

The rainy days don't last forever.
Sometimes my mind and anxiety try to convince me it's the latter.
To be happy is a life's mission, my most precious goal and desire.
But when you struggle with anxiety it can seem as if it's like trying to
contain fire.
"Stop crying, suck it up, stop being so weak,"
Are the common things people get told by those who have no
understanding.
To have your body lash out in such a way can be scary.
It can be very overwhelming even when you're aware of what is
happening.
But you are not alone, remember to breathe and take it slow.
Take a deep breath, close your eyes, and let it go.
Know you are a powerful and courageous force.
You are as mighty as a lion with a warrior's soul.
Give yourself credit for all that you do,
Because if somebody ever stepped in your shoes, they could never see
it through.
Happiness is real and so is peace.
These are obtainable fruits and you are deserving.
These are things you have to commit to growing and nourishing.
So keep on smiling and keep on fighting.
Fuck the peanut gallery in your head because they know nothing.
You are the conductor of your own mind and body,

You set the tone and have the power to override them!

Mind Over Matter.

I am safe. I am loved. I am love.
I wash out the little voices telling me it's none of the above.
They don't know about this life of mine and how far I've come.
I deserve to smile. To have peace and fully feel joy.
I am safe. I am loved. I am love.
I wash out the little voices saying otherwise, They are not welcome
anymore.
It is my birthright to embrace my desires and dreams.
I am strong. I am resilient. I am mighty like the lion.
I am not my past. I am not my trauma.
I have the ability and right to transform however I desire.
I have died what feels like a thousand times over.
But through death comes rebirth,
New life and new soil.
I am strong. I am love. I am loved.
I am the rose that grew from concrete,
The lotus out of the mud.

Breakdowns for Breakthroughs.

I've been coming to so many realizations and understandings.
Healing isn't linear and some hurts require extra loving.
Sometimes the grief comes out to be seen and caressed by the moon's luminescence.
My tears wash over and cleanse the wounds I cannot see, but I feel them.
I hold them and nourish them letting them know it's okay.
My soul cries tears of joy and release for the girl gone,
Buried and baptized away.
For all the trials and tribulations she had to endure and overcome.
My angels helped me pull on my inner reserves, strength, and resilience.
On most days it felt like I would never find my way.
And although I didn't understand the reason for those days,
I now see that my journey has allowed me to be here and to expand.
In this space filled with balance, peace, and acceptance,
Once a queen whose crown had been dismantled and trampled.
Her wings weighed heavy and she lost the urge to fly,
But the woman who has been reborn not only flies but she thrives.
She looks at her former self in awe and deep respect,
It was the power of her ancestors that rose her time and time again.
Breakdowns for breakthroughs understand it isn't over yet.
So much story left unwritten and the best is what is next.

Growing Pains Pt. 1.

No, I won't give up or tap out this go-round.
I'll put my pants on one leg at a time.
I will do my best to work through the motions, through these
emotions.
I am growing.
It hurts like hell but I know that it's worth it.
I have to fight the good fight to get to where I'm going.
I am constantly shedding and evolving.
Discovering myself along this powerful and sacred journey.
I just need a second to calm my thoughts and catch my footing.
I call upon my ancestors to help with this transition.
I will be okay. I will find my center.
I am not lost. I am just growing through the motions.
These growing pains just let me know I'm getting closer to wholeness.
Pick yourself up and dust yourself off my love.
Wipe the tears from your eyes and pick your head up.
It's okay, it's raining hard on your parade.
Pretty baby just take a deep breath, the rainbow is on its way.
Has anyone ever told you you're all you'll ever need?
You are perfectly imperfect I wish you could see.
You are the empress, a divine being.
You are more than enough please believe it.
You are love and light in all of your essence.
You are soft and you are rare, you are not your trespasses.

SEYLAH LOVE

I know your heart is tired, I know you want to go cold.
I know you want to give up but please believe in better tomorrows.
You're losing your faith I know but please don't let the world steal your
joy.
You are all that is good and pure in this world.
Your heart is your greatest superpower, please don't build that wall.
Feel what you feel and take your baby steps forward.
Cry your tears and leave them where they fall.
Listen to your heart, follow the voice of your soul.
Please pretty baby.
Hear out this call.
Love yourself like the love you've been desperately searching for.

Growing Pains Pt. 2.

What am I doing with my life?
Is a question I've asked myself over a thousand times...
Is this right? Is this the right way?
I'm too afraid of failing. I can't make any mistakes.
"You're almost 20"
Yeah but what does that mean?
Because last time I checked there are people in their 40s still asking the
same questions as me.
Does entering my twenties mean I'm supposed to have it all together?
Does that mean now I have to pretend there aren't bad days and
stormy weather?
Because If so I don't think I want to sign that silent agreement.
Be done school at this one, but make sure no kids before here.
There's all these unrealistic expectations and time frames people assign
to just living.
Society makes it seem like our lives are supposed to reflect what they
say is ideal,
But it's all a setup to keep your spirit confined and unaware.
It's all societal constructs and I say Grow at your own pace.
Listen to what your soul craves and let that guide you to your passions
and purpose.
Make mistakes, ask for help, and release the guilt and shame they
program within this.
Finish school when you finish and have kids when you're ready.

SEYLAH LOVE

Scream and shout in tears if it's needed.
Know that your reality can be whatever you desire.
So do yourself a favor say fuck it and ground your dreams into this
beautiful world of ours.
Move at your own pace and do what's best for you.
Live for you and only you and let your spirit lead you higher in truth.

From the Cocoon She Emerges.

Been sitting in silence getting to know me.
She's been teaching and showing me a lot about my Truth these days.
She's been helping me understand who I really am underneath all of
the projections and suffocating expectations.
Under the trauma, pain, anxiety, and depression.
Guiding me along my inner and outer journeys,
showing me how I want to be loved, and how I need to be nourished.
Not only by others but by my own mind, body, and spirit.
She's showing me how to nurture my inner child with compassion and
patience.
I can no longer focus on the mundane I say,
I have too much life asking to be enjoyed and experienced.
To much important work I have to do for myself and the collective.
She is my very best friend, my confidant, she's my number one Lover.
I found out I'm stronger than I could have ever imagined.
Soul with the force of lighting and thunder.
I've fallen in love with myself and this time it is forever.
Magical and mystical I am, my pure essence.
I burned the shackles binding me and let my wings free to stretch high
and touch the Heavens.
I held the keys and way to freedom all along,
Deep down inside I was always close to Home.

Past.

It's December 18th, 2021 and it's 11:48 pm and I'm editing my playlist with my baby yelling let that shit run DJ. I am alive. I am grateful and I am so joyful in this beautiful moment. I have sworn to give my life my unconditional presence and love. That means being fully committed to moments like this that are full of beauty, peace, and bliss. I've often deprived myself of moments like this out of fear that they wouldn't last long. Fearing the ever changing flow of life. So intolerant of anything that wasn't pleasurable because all I'd come to know was pain and suffering. I hid away as far as I could from my shadow, my demons and the dark side of the moon but running away from the night doesn't stop it from coming. Everything has its natural order and rhythm in our lives. Everything cycles. Everything is born and everything dies. That is the way it is and it is meant to be. Sometimes we have to die to recover parts of ourselves and our being just like how in rebirth we must kill anything that stunts our life and ability to grow and stretch into a new level of self, consciousness, self-discovery, and healing. Nobody ever promised blooming would be easy and that's something I remind myself every day of my life. Anything that isn't growing is dead so I'd rather take the discomfort and temporary growing pains over no life and no breath at all. I have come to a deeper understanding of life and its ways and in taking the time to do so I've also come to gain a more intimate understanding of myself. I've gotten clearer on what life means to me, and what I WANT to make of it. I feel like nowadays we kind of underestimate the importance of figuring out those things out. It's what gives us direction I believe. We have so much power over ourselves and our lives than we allow ourselves to see at times. Love is infinite. Happiness, joy, wellness, and peace are things we must work towards, invest in, and dedicate and commit ourselves to. Sometimes it isn't easy because life has a way of throwing all kinds of curve balls and obstacles but it's in these that we can apply all we've learned and show ourselves and life that we are capable. It is in those challenges that we gain gems of wisdom and become more fortified and refined on every level. They expose us to deeper layers of ourselves and help us understand what we are made of. I feel more times often than not we find that we are much more stronger, courageous, capable, and resilient than we give ourselves credit for. Lately, I've come to have this beautiful movie view of my life and I've never been filled with so much gratitude as I am now. I've been crying tears of joy, relief, and gratitude a lot lately. I've stopped to take it all in and appreciate how far I've come and how amazing I am. No matter how uncomfortable or unpleasant my experiences have been, I have also had brilliant ones and both have helped me become the person I am today. I find peace and acceptance in what has happened. I've learned from the painful and unfortunate experiences and carry the ones that have been nothing short of glorious with me always. I do not have to become my pains, nor do I have to inflict them continuously on myself and over my life. I can always create moments full of glory, joy, and deep love whenever I choose. I choose forward movement and I choose me. I choose spirit and I choose love. I am a sovereign being and I have the power and authority to orchestrate and live my life as I please. I look at myself in the mirror and see child me, adolescent me, and teen me and they no longer look or feel like strangers. I finally feel them blended within me, resting safely at home. I have never seen or felt myself and my being so clearly. I've always felt so cracked, scattered, and unreal my whole life and now I feel so put together. I've fought and advocated so hard for myself and I'm so grateful that I never gave up. I feel like I'm finally stepping into my womanhood and embracing my skin in a way I've always dreamed of. I finally feel free and I have no one but Spirit to thank for that. It's been a long journey for me and I'm so used to people undermining what I've been through and how far I've come that for the longest time I was doing it to myself. Then one day I looked in the mirror and decided enough was enough. I realized I don't need anyone outside of me to validate or acknowledge my journey, pain or growth. I know what I've gone through and I know where I've been and that's enough. I know who I am and I don't need anyone to cosign that. I don't need to prove myself or convince anyone of anything. I am my own woman and this is my life. The Divines witnessing eyes and approving heart are all I need. I see me, I choose me and I unconditionally love and value me. Here's to growth, healing, life, and love.

She Breathes.

I breathe and it feels as though it's for the first time.
I've figured out how to keep my balance this time around.
How to play in the clouds but still land softly on the ground.
I've found a peace of mind and reconnected to the Queen inside my
crown.
By not living for anyone but me, myself and I.
By leaving the past in the past and giving myself the gift of a new life.
I've found a peace of mind and I will maintain it.
I brought the color back into my life and I see it in 20/20 vision.
The Divine breathed life back into me after laying the old me to rest.
I feel peaceful.
I feel alive.
I am searingly present.

She Believes and It Shall Be.

It was at that moment at 9:34 a.m. she believed in herself.
She believes in believing and she believes that she will accomplish her
dreams one day.
She believes she has what it takes.
She knows she will be great one day.
Mark my words her soul says,
She promises her poetry will touch millions of hearts one day.

I Direct it.

To stand in my truth and never feel guilty,
Is a pleasure I've had the honor of partaking.
I've been stuck under the mold of what I was told I should be.
Growing into my own skin has been awkward but such a gift to me.
To watch and feel myself grow into a new form of my being,
To not live for validation or anybody's acceptance.
To live and thrive off of my own love, compassion, and affection.
My own admiration and validation,
To be proud of my own self-image.
No more conforming.
Fuck society and its hidden agendas they don't control me.
At the end of the story when the sun sets in my finale,
Only I have to look back and accept the makings of my story.
It would be a shame to look back and be filled with regret,
At seeing a life that was never truly lived for oneself.
To see a body and soul that never had a chance to love themselves,
Guided by other people's fears and selfish narratives.
So I say no more living for anybody else.
No more moldings. I'm done. No more S on my chest.
It's my movie. I direct it, and I WILL tell my story.
Good bye black and white,
Hello technicolor.
What a honor it it is, to be alive in living color.

Peace of Mind.

Peace.

It lives within me.

Growing up I never thought it could befriend me.

So used to screaming, so used to chaos —there was always turmoil.

The thoughts always rushing in as I struggled to quiet it all.

My emotions run so deep that everybody I meet feels like a part of me.

A reflection, a lesson, a message for me to receive.

In every smile, every tear, and every eye.

Reminding me that everything has a place and purpose within time.

My inner child and I hold each other's hands when we're feeling low.

We let each other know how loved,

How needed, and how wanted we truly are.

We're teaching each other how to find homes in ourselves first.

How to be patient and extend us grace and compassion.

How love is really everlasting and oh so powerful.

Unbeknownst to me she's been trying to guide me back to wholeness and peace.

I am grateful I finally gave her the opportunity to be my guide across the sea.

I am so grateful to love and be loved by her so deeply.

She has guided me through the dark and helped me find my inner way.

There's peace, there's quiet and there's purpose in me.

I planted it, nourished it, and watched it grow as mighty as the oak tree.

SOMETIMES I LIE AWAKE AT NIGHT

Here's to Healing. Here's to Peace and Here's to Sovereignty.
I changed the direction in which I pour and my heart has never
known a love so warm.
I'm learning how to shield and protect my energy from others.
How to trust my intuition and how to utilize my discernment.
How to not overload my system and stay centered and balanced on all
levels.
How to tame my anxiety when it's fighting to get its way.
How to know when I've done enough emotionally and when to step
away.
And dare I say it how to enforce my boundaries.
How to find a balance of giving because I'm the queen of
overextending.
I used to let my emotions get the best of me.
I'd break down and fall into pieces trying to get people to see the
worth in me.
Now I speak my peace and keep it moving.
If they don't see me for the Love that I am then that's their problem.
Learning how to pick and choose my battles in this chapter has been
so important.
Familiarizing myself with my Independence has been my favorite
lesson along this journey.
Unapologetically stepping into my light and power and expressing it.
Honoring my autonomy and the ode that I took,
To have and to hold me until death do us part.

The Little Things.

It's the way the birds play in the trees in the early morning.
One by one they sing their songs to me.
It's the way the leaves dance in the wind telling secrets.
They've spent years growing and learning the ancient melodies of this
planet.
It's how beautiful the sky looks in the early mornings.
It's my favorite R&B songs at dawn when I'm yearning.
I sing for me, for my soul and our release.
It's the little things like this that fill me with bliss.
A soft smile.
A loving glance.
The way your lover's hand feels on your skin.
The random I love yous and the surprise kisses.
How warm your favorite sweater feels in the late night winters.
Little things leave big imprints,
They're chicken noodle soup for the spirit.
But it's also the little things we seem to ignore the most.
I hope one day we grow to appreciate the little things just a bit more.

Love Your Skin.

You are beautiful because you are you and not them.
You are beautiful because you are in the skin you are in.
You are beautiful because you are uniquely created.
There are no mistakes my love you were perfectly orchestrated.
Fuck society and anyone who doesn't speak life over your being.
Fuck them, their opinions and projections.
You are beautiful no matter what they say.
Focus on you and growing love from within.
Because remember comparison is truly the thief of joy in the end.

Love Will Get Us Home.

My brothers and my sisters we all come from one,
Oblivion; a place of death and creation.
Where everything and nothing exist as one.
In its arms we can find comfort lying under the stars.
As we dream about the galaxies our spirits are exstenions of,
We remember the times when Love and unity was the reason.
When we all sat together, hand in hand in integration.
Building worlds of wonder through the power of our hearts pure
creations.
We come here to remember, to be and embody. .
We come here to experience life and the expansiveness of our soul's
essence.
We come here to see God in all of their different expressions,
So that we remember the ability to create heaven on Earth is at the tip
of our fingers.
The key is to remember a sweet and simple truth,
That Love is the alpha, omega and savior.

The Everlasting Tree.

The growing tree, the giving tree.
With its arms spread wide it stands alone reaching to the sky.
While the sun silently nourishes and feeds what we cannot see.
The growing tree, the giving tree stands firm and tall.
The wind runs its fingers through its leaves one by one caressing and
nurturing each.
The giving tree, the growing tree has grown a little weak.
The strength she once possessed seems to be giving way to the darkness
that seems to always be hovering in the distance.
The dark clouds linger waiting for its time to devour the power that is
inside,
Trying to destroy the foundation the giving tree, the growing tree has
spent so much time building..
The giving tree the growing tree comes from a special seed.
One that exemplifies strength and power, a willful, resilient one
indeed.
No matter how much rain or how many storms come its way,
Its roots will stay strong and firm day to day.
This is a foundation, a spirit no one can break.
Arms raised praising the Heavens and roots planted deep in the Earth,
reminding her she's forever loved, held down, and abundant.
The sun wraps its arms around the tree lovingly, washing her with
power and courage.
Shining its love and its warmth over her, nourishing every fiber of her

being.
Reminding her that she has everything she already needs.
She has all the tools to continue growing and flourishing,
For she is the giving tree, the growing tree.
Ready and prepared for anything.

Ancestral Veneration: The Rising and Reclamation

I have all the force I need in me.

I am strong, I am courageous, I am otherworldly.

The power and resilience inside of me,

reigns from generations of women who have cried out in rage and suffering.

For many years my people have fought to find peace.

Now is the time to finish what they started.

To break old patterns, walls, and beliefs,

We're fighting for better days and this time they're here for eternity.

We'll reclaim what was stolen, robbed and tarnished.

Awakening sleeping dragons and hidden knowledge.

I know that they live in me and through me, they work.

The same blood pumping through my veins we are all one.

So much fierceness runs through our hearts.

Black girl magick isn't just a phrase around these parts.

It's time to put in the work to bring healing to the root of us.

To create better days, better ways, and something brighter.

We'll prepare our babies, show and teach them better.

My ancestors guide me, my divine intelligence.

I know that I am not and never will be alone as I travel.

Through me they move, see and get active.

The noxious waters are drying up, no more will we be imprisoned.

SEYLAH LOVE

The dark days must go, there's no mercy for the wicked.
It's time for a beautiful summer, no more bondage and oppression.
Step but step, Brick by brick,
I am a new beginning for my lineage.
One that knows no ends, no walls, or limitations.
We will rise to greatness and they will feel our thunder.
These words are our power and through them we'll move mountains.
Ring the alarms, the revolution has started.

Present.

I woke up this morning and felt as if I could fly. As if I could birth an entire world and nation and take care of it with ease and poise. I woke up feeling so deeply in tune with my body and the sacred feminine within me. I have been prioritizing simplicity these days, more than I ever have in my entire life. I've realized a lot of the things that were complicating my life were outdated thought processes, fear, doubt, and insecurity. These things were causing me to act, perceive and think in ways that were contradictory to what my soul genuinely felt and needed. They would cause me to separate like oil and water. I have decided to pour all of the oil out and be sustained and nourished only by the water.. I want harmony. I want unity. I want truth and I want love. And I can cultivate that for myself at any given moment through the intentional acts and prayers I give form to in my life through my words, essence and soul-filled presence and expression.

This phase and cycle of my life is all about me and the Divine. It's about me no longer silencing myself to keep the peace or minimizing myself and my dreams to appease other people so that they can feel better regarding the level of mediocrity or negativity they are performing at and living through. I won't silence my truth anymore so that others can feel more comfortable living in their illusions and lies. I didn't come here to be mediocre or live a fear based life. I came here to spark, inspire, and revolutionize and that starts with me being okay being the rebel misfit I was born to be. We align with our destiny through intense focus on what is real, life-giving and sustaining, while making self-honoring choices that align us with our highest expression, aspirations and dreams. It requires much persistence, determination, discipline and resilience. Even if the methods or means change in different seasons the purpose stays the same. To love, spark, inspire, and revolutionize.

I deeply understand now that to be a leader, a visionary, and a true revolutionary you have to be okay with going against the grain and doing things in your own unique and divinely led way. No matter how crazy it looks to the outside world. To pave a new way you have to be willing to travel, gather, build and grow alone sometimes. You have to be willing to answer the call whenever the Divine rings. You have to be confident in sharing it all with the world. To me, the most sacred parts of the process is the traveling and gathering stages. The act of going through many different experiences, and traveling to many different places internally and externally to gather what is necessary for the build and creation that'll then lead up to "the curtain call" moments of life. Those peak moments in our lives where the gathering, building, and embodying is complete and what has grown and been created is now ready to be witnessed on the grand stage of Life. Practice is over and a masterful show is now ready to go on. A big bang of cosmic creation. Sometimes it's something being birthed within the spirit that can be witnessed and touched by you and only you and sometimes it's things we birth into the physical that the world around us can witness, engage with, and touch. I believe these often mark pivotal and life-changing moments for us that we know we will never be the same after but know we will forever be better and grateful for.

My inner child and I are deeply secure in who we are now and what we are meant to do. We have become unshakeable and indestructible, no longer easily moved or triggered by the outside world. We only ascribe to divinely fueled and led things now, and that means fear, doubt, and insecurity are things we can no longer know or entertain. The process of journeying and wandering for our souls' evolution and development is something I have truly, truly fallen in love with. I don't care to simply just arrive anymore. I care about the process of it and all of the soul lessons, experiences, life, and love in between. We can arrive at places many times in our lives but the things we encounter and experience in the in-between are often things that cannot be easily duplicated or replicated. And those are the moments I live for.

I'm forever leaving behind those old paradigms where fear and doubt ruled me. I no longer fear change, death, pain, challenges, or the valleys. I no longer fear myself. I know that I have the power and ability through the Divine, my Holy Mother and Father to see it through, rise and learn. I don't have to over-identify with the happenings of my life anymore to feel it has meaning. I don't have to cling and hold on to the stories in an attempt to feel like I and my life have purpose. My life has meaning and purpose simply because I am. Me being and embodying is enough and all I need to do. I am a simple traveler and observer. A bee, willing to go to each flower to harvest, grow, learn, and experience with gracefulness, poise, and innocence. Grateful just to be alive and be a part of this world and the lives of those who I love and who love me. I don't wish to "have" or "possess" anything anymore. I just want to experience, witness, and embrace with deep love, respect, honor and humility.

It is time for me to go. It is time for me to share myself with the world and to let the world share itself with me in an open, honest, true, and tender way. I'm ready to be vulnerable and intimate with the world and I'm ready for it to be vulnerable and intimate with me. I'm ready to witness others with love, tenderness, and deep reverence the same way I desire them to do with me. I'm not afraid of loss anymore because I now know that it doesn't exist. It is nothing short of an illusion that distorts us and the way we see and understand on this Earthly plane. We can never lose what is of us, only if we give it away. We can only experience with deep presence, pure love, and respect, and let things go when it is time. But in truth, we can never lose it forever or even at all, because it will always be in and with our soul. The things that experience will forever be a part of us unless we chose them not to be in which we have the autonomy and power to do so. We don't have to keep what we do not want. We can always burn away or release what we do not deem healthy, supportive or nourishing. It is always in our right to do so as it is up to our discretion only. We are here to dance with and embrace the outward physical manifestation of the goodness, love, light, and other soul aspects that are us. And even if the physical thing itself has gone, it will always remain with you and a part of you because it is you to an extent. This is the Oneness and the interconnectedness of all.

I'm ready to experience the more lighthearted and divine aspects of me. I'm done living and wading in the shadows as I've made peace with all that was hidden and held captive and secret there. I no longer see myself through these things because I have taken them and returned them home into the light and now I wish to live, see, and experience it all differenly. I wish to see myself through the genius, magick, and majesticness of other pure, honest, and true souls. I wish to be inspired, sparked, and revolutionized through them and the world now because I have learned how to experience and witness most purely and as selflessly as possible. I understand and see love so much more clearly now and I'm ready to get away from things, places, and people that do not because they are a liability to my freedom, heart, and soul. I'm ready for others who will grow with me, stretch with me, and love me and to have others around me who are on the same soul plane, with the same intentions to simply be an activist of Love in whatever way their soul deems fit for them. I'm ready to only engage with things that nourish, spark, and excite my soul and to live a prosperous life full of these things. And so it is.

Seylah Loves Emancipation.

Freedom at last, freedom at last.
Freedom from the shackles and binds that kept me trapped inside my
mind.
Freedom from the shackles and binds that kept my heart and spirit
blind.
Freedom from the shackles and binds that kept my body weak and
petrified.
Oh glory be to God, I've escaped from the cage and became the
butterfly.
Free of the shackles ready to stretch, expand and fly.
Free of the shackles that left my heart closed and confined.
Freedom at last, freedom at last.
Freedom from the cage that kept my voice locked away.
Freedom from the cage that kept my truth and power at bay.
Freedom from the cage that kept my heart in dismay.
Oh Glory be to God, the caged bird does sing.
Free of the cage that told the bird there was no way,
That they could never fly and touch the skies that were made for them
to play.
I lay the past to rest and pay my last respects.
As I cry my last tears for those black and white years.
No regrets, no shame, no guilt or pity.
Everything happened as it should've,

SEYLAH LOVE

Twas the journey of my becoming.
I honor and venerate every past form of my being,
As they've all played an important part in the process of my freeing.
I look back on the past with peace, love and acceptance,
As I make my way to everything I only then could have imagined
With death comes new life, new soil and creation
Oh Glory be to God it's Seylah Love's emancipation.

Her Prayer 9;23.

Where is your God now they say?
Where is this savior that you say promised you peace and a life of
savory?
Where is this God they say?
If he was really listening why does he have you out here suffering this
way?
Where is your God they say?
They laugh and they gossip about your trials and tribulations.
My God, I say
Is in the air, in the magic of every breath I take.
My God, I say
Isn't in the money, but in the joy and wonder that always surrounds
me.
My God, I say
Is in the strength and will that fills me on the days when my knees
quake.
My God, I say
Is in the words of gratitude and praise that I sing every day.
They say how come your God hasn't come to save you yet?
I laugh and say have you not seen the way he has raised me time and
time again?
Have you not seen the way I've beaten every oppressor that comes to
take my heart and soul away?
Have you not seen the vision he has blessed me with?

SEYLAH LOVE

The vision that will anchor a new lineage and leave an imprint on the
world that the people will never forget?
I say you judge whether or not a person has God by the wrong things.
By how much money, clothes, and physical abundance they have to
their name.
That is not how you know a Being has God I say.
You know by the fruits that grow from the eternal soul within.
Joy. Peace. Temperance and Self Control.
Kindness, Goodness, Faithfulness, and Gentleness.
These are the aspects of a God-driven and soul-filled person.
You laugh and grin but I must ask...
How would you know if I have any of these things for myself,
If all you do is mock, judge, and take joy in,
the apparent struggle and suffering of others?
Dare I say it, you may be missing a couple of fruits of your own,
If you feel joy and pleasure looking down on another person's soul.
My God is in my hope, my faithfulness and resilience.
My God is in the blood of my ancestors, I am their prayers incarnated.
My God is in all of the wisdom, knowledge, and healing I have
obtained.
As I have traveled a path, created and anointed in Jesus's name.
My God is in these words that I write and share,
In the hopes of sparking change, revolution, and healing in his name.
My God is in the testimonies that I share to inspire.
My God is in the way I am of service to others.
My God is the invisible force that walks with and protects me.
That cannot be seen or heard in material objects or superficiality.
My God is in the truth I speak and anchor myself in consciously.
My God is in the compassion, gentleness, and wisdom I share with
those on a daily.
My God is in the flame that burns endlessly within me,
The eternal light that fuels my being and keeps my soul going.

SOMETIMES I LIE AWAKE AT NIGHT

That is my God, my Savior, and my very best friend.
So you may laugh, slander, and gossip all you please,
But dear one I hope you understand now how God filled I really am.
I am guided in ways you could never ever understand.
Unless you are too truly guided by the same holy hands.
I am so abundant in love, joy, truth, and peace.
And it is my faithfulness that keeps my cup full in every single
moment.
You can laugh, mock, and try to rob me of what's inside,
but you can never take the Love, Wonder, and Favor that God showers
over my life.
So I must sit here and curiously ask,
Do you think God would respect the way you laugh at, condemn, and
judge his children?
Don't worry about me, worry about you and your lack of union.
Worry about your life and your priorities because I promise I'm not
one of them.
You're too busy worrying about what God is doing for me,
that you're blocking your blessings and connection to him.
Worry about filling up your cup with something other than judgment,
envy, and wickedness.
So the next time you dare ask where someone's God is in hopes of
laughing,
Look into your cup first and address what fruits are missing.

I Left it at the Altar.

Leave it all at the altar and give it to us.
My ancestors whisper as they feel the weight of my grievances
threatening to erupt.
Leave it all at the altar and give it to us.
My ancestors whisper as thunderous wails escape from all four corners
of my heart.
Leave it all at the altar and give it to us.
My ancestors whisper, as I fall to my knees and beg for relief, strength,
and mercy.
The pain heavies and overwhelms my flesh.
Every breath feels grueling, like a knife through the chest.
My bones are weakened, my body numb,
As I violently release mounds of grief and sorrow.
Leave it all at the altar and give it to us.
I open up my bible and turn to Psalms 20 & 21.
I get on my knees and raise my head to the heavens,
I pray for protection, relief, divine grace, and salvation
Leave it at the altar and give it to us.
I feel my ancestors lay hands over my body and heart,
As I give sound to the wounds that have left bruises on my Spirit.
As my cries and tears tell the tales of all of my trials and tribulations.
Leave it at the altar and give it to us.
Let us cleanse you with our love and with the love of the Holy Spirit.
Let your tears run down and let it out to us.

SOMETIMES I LIE AWAKE AT NIGHT

We hear you, we see you, and it is in us you can trust.
Let us carry you when you are meek and hold you when you are weak,
For we have wailed the same song that your heart does speak.
Leave it at the altar and give it to us.
Knees aching, eyes swollen but heart light as a feather.
They uplift me, empower me, and raise me with their love,
While reminding me of my strength and the power in my blood.
Prayer is powerful, it's our soul's greatest medicine.
It can remedy the toughest of wounds and soothe the deepest of
grievances.
It grounds me deeply in the love and support of my ancestors,
As I leave it at the altar and give it to them and Great Spirit.
I left it at the altar and gave it to my ancestors,
And I watched them ease my pains, calm my mind, and relax my spirit.
I left it at the altar and gave it to my ancestors,
And I watched them turn my tears into powerful Holy Medicine.
I left it at the altar and gave it to my ancestors,
And I watched them carry my grievances off into the Heavens,
Wrapped in my prayers, their love and protection.

I Smile.

I smile because I deserve joy.
For every lashing on my soul, I've promised myself to fill the cracks
with gold.
Look at her—,
beautifully twisted and haunted.
I smile for all the times I had the love ripped out of my heart.
Through the cracks my soul glimmers and whispers tales of hope.
For I smile for all the times the void swallowed me whole.
I smile because my face has known more tears than the sun's glow.
My body has known more aches and pains than the gentle caress of
love and hope.
I smile for all the times I have been so terribly misunderstood.
For all of the dagger wounds in my back left from the words of every
reaper's ill tongue.
She smiles they say, how can she smile this way? Has she not had
enough yet? Does she need more pain to blow out her flame?
How dare she beam in faith this way?
With the lord's words engraved all over her chest and face.
I smile for every ancestor who shares with me in this breath.
For every whip that beat the smile and freedom from off of their
backs.
I smile because I am loved and I deserve the very best.
For every time my love was violently stolen from my womb and my
breast.

SOMETIMES I LIE AWAKE AT NIGHT

I smile because joy becomes me more than stress and duress.
For every attack that thrashed chaotically all over my mind and spirit.
I smile because I chose faith over the fear of the wicked.
And because I know that every tongue and hand that has bruised my
skin will succumb to the very iniquity that moved them to do me in.
I smile because I'm a heavyweight champ.
I've never backed down but my thighs show the remnants of the silent
fights I didn't win.
I smile because I still have more life and breath within,
and as long as I get another day I'll continue to find a thousand
reasons to smile because love will always win in the end.

Heavy But Blessed is the Head.

Heavy is the head that wears the crown and the soul that is just and is led by righteousness.

Heavy is the head that follows the calling of the unknown as it creates and builds new worlds out of faith and stone.

Patience is a virtue. One that demands presence, absolute trust, and belief in a vision God given. It is patience and faith that supports us in carrying every stone and provision.

Heavy is the head that wears the crown and the soul that is led by righteousness.

Heavy is the head and the heart that follows the path of soulful ordinance. That follows not the path of societal expectation but that of the one and only king and queen, the Holy Spirit.

Blessed be the child that can carry their own.

That bears the burden of being the new beginning with the intention to flush out the poison and break the chains that the oppressors and colonizers have given.

Heavy is the head that dares to dwell between life and death.

That dares to bear the responsibility of giving life to new generations and tend to the soul where our ancestors primed and wept.

Blessed be the child that can carry their own.

That is first on the front line when the red cardinal signals war.

When the systems of oppression that serve the wicked line up at our doors,

SOMETIMES I LIE AWAKE AT NIGHT

Demanding we dual to the death— as they come for our life, our spirit
and sacred breath.
Blessed be the child that can carry their own.
The child that chooses to love and anchor themselves in the Divine's
word.

Cosmic Musing #1:
The Gift of Growing Pains

Sometimes I lie awake at night and think about how grateful I am for growing pains. I have reached a place in my journey and development where I have gotten extremely comfortable and familiar with the process and cycle of spiritual deaths and rebirths. I've been able to identify the different phases and steps better, which has allowed me to become more intimately engaged with the overall process on both ends. I have found that the dying part energetically and spiritually speaking is easier for me. It's easier for me to let go, submerge into the void, and be in a state of rest, stillness, and release. It has become pleasurable and extremely sensual to me. I enjoy the shedding and becoming lighter on every level because I've spent so much of my life feeling weighed down. So the dying and releasing is something I happily partake in, it's the rebirthing process that is taking me a while to get used to. The phase of coming back to life can be extremely difficult and challenging for me because of the growing pains and blindness that come with it. That part where you feel extremely naked and everything feels foreign and unrecognizable. Where you see yourself in the mirror but don't quite fully feel secure in the face looking back at you because it is an entirely new you. That awkward phase of regrowing into yourself and new spiritual skin because this is a version of you you've never experienced before and you have to figure out how to be in it, move in it, and embody it. It feels like hitting puberty again but on an internal and spiritual level while your body is just the vessel that allows your spirit to go through the process in a very physical and visceral way. Something that helps me surrender to the process and find a greater sense of ease, peace, and comfortability in it is shifting the way I think about and perceive growing pains. Giving them a more positive definition instead of looking at it as something daunting and strenuous.

Growing pains is a term that I'm sure the majority of the world is familiar with and I'm positive that almost everyone in the world has experienced and gone through them at various points throughout life. First, we go through death where we have major releases and give final farewells to things inside and out. Then we are planted into new soil where we are often watered by the rains of the showers that come and go as we are shedding and purging. As we are nestled in Gaias temple we get to that place where the rain fully ceases and the sun comes out allowing us to finally get some peace within the darkness and coolness of this new soil. As the Sun shines on us, it then becomes time to sprout. It becomes time to break through the protective encasing and soil that held and protected us as we transitioned so that we can finally bloom wide and free for all to see and witness. This is where the growing pains come in. Where now we are being asked to be uncomfortable and maybe even isolated for a little while for the sake of allowing ourselves to grow and become anew. Where we were once comfortable being cradled by the soil and the quiet peace it held, we find ourselves having to go against it as we anchor new roots downward and push ourselves up, through, and out and that shit can hurt. It can hurt to stretch after being cradled and wrapped up for so long. It can sting as you expand. It can be frazzling and intimidating because who knows what is going to be on the surface when you push through? Who knows how the Earth will respond to the new you or what these new environments and experiences will be like? Who knows what this new version of you will be like or how it will feel? It's the unknown that can be daunting on our minds even though our souls know that everything will be perfectly okay. Sometimes there will be an internal dissonance because oftentimes our souls will be excited and joyful, giddy like a child the night before the first day of school— while our minds will be filled with worry, full of what ifs fueled by not knowing and the lack of control we have during the process of entering a new life cycle, soul cycle and level within Earth school. Often as we are being reborn our minds immediately want to know every detail of every step no matter how impractical and unrealistic it is and this is where I often have trouble. My desire for control and to know everything sometimes makes it damn near insufferable to be reborn. Sometimes my desire to rush just so I can see, makes it difficult for me to be present and to surrender to the process even though in my heart of hearts I know all will be well. Sometimes my mind gets stuck on the discomfort and temporary growing pains that come with coming back to life and all I can think about is how awkward and exposed I feel to everything instead of how free and alive I also feel. Sometimes my mind tries to convince me that all I'll ever be is the growing pains itself and that this new chapter and cycle of life will be just like the rest. I realized that my mind is the thing trying to demonize and contort something that is meant to be a beautiful sign of Life, Magic, and Evolution into something scary, painful, and torturous. It wasn't until I was able to shift my perspective of growing pains and allow myself to see it as a beautiful byproduct of the sacred process of Creation on a spiritual and physical level did things change.

It is so amazing and powerful to be able to give birth to yourself over and over and through this understanding and perspective shift, I was able to form a better relationship with Life, Death, and the sacred feminine within. I was looking at the growing pains from a limiting, fearful, and fixed standpoint, instead of looking at it from a higher, neutral, and expansive one. Growing pains are not to be mistaken for suffering or torture. Suffering is not and does not have to be something that inherently comes with growing, expanding, and going through the death/rebirth process overall. Yes, these life and spiritual transitions and transformations we go through can be a shock to our systems and can sometimes be difficult to traverse, but we have to believe in our ability to show up, support, and take care of ourselves. We have to trust that we are fully capable of riding the wave without drowning and know it's okay to crawl before we walk until we get more familiarized and comfortable with the change(s). A baby cries upon initially being born. They experience a huge shock from one moment being wrapped peacefully in the womb, to all of a sudden being pushed through the canal (for us as adults valleys) into a new, unfamiliar environment, with limbs and a body they have yet to get to know. They cry because it is uncomfortable and scary and maybe even a bit frustrating but that cry is a sign of life. It's a sign that they have safely made it alive and with breath. Our tears, our breath, our movements, and those growing pains let us know we are alive and it is a testament to how magnificent creation is. It reminds us that anything dead does not grow. It doesn't breathe. It doesn't cry. It doesn't move. They are a sign that we still have so much potential left to explore and express. It's a sign that we still have more life left to live, more experiences to be immersed in, and more chapters to write. Those growing pains are a sign that we made it to the other side and a testament to how far we have come physically and spiritually. It's a testament to how powerful, strong, and courageous we are inside and out because we chose to undergo this process even through the aches and fears. It's a testament to our resilience because we chose to undergo the process so that we can continue to not only grow but heal, love, live, and be despite the challenges and obstacles that tried to stop us and take us out. It's a testament to the many times we said yes to life even during the times we wanted to say no. It's a testament to the many times we continued to fight even when we didn't want to and how even through the pain of the pushes and the tears and sweat that came with them we continued to preserve. A testament to how we kept pushing, fighting, hoping, and believing until we broke through and made it through to the other side.

Every time we are reborn we are breathing new air, and feeling new life, and just like a baby seeks the comforts of their mother, we too have to seek the comfort of the Divine Mother.. The way flowers seek the comfort of Mother Gaia, we have to seek comfort in the divine mothers and sacred feminine within who will help us work through and get through the process with as little strain, stress, and difficulty as possible. Mother Mayu governs all cosmic wombs and is the mother of the Milky Way. When we are in the process of death and rebirth it is her arms and her milk that we look to for nourishment, nurturance, and warmth. It is her, the Divine Mother, and Gaia's loving embrace that holds us, supports us, and helps us integrate and embody the new version of ourselves. Through Mayu's cosmic midwifery and Gaia's doulas, we can give birth to ourselves and tend to the newly born us with deep tenderness, patience, compassion and love. Gaia teaches us that growing pains are something to be celebrated and can be pleasurable, exciting, and exhilarating if we allow it to be. We see that as winter turns into spring. The fact that we as souls can give birth to ourselves over and over is such a phenomenal thing and wouldn't be possible without the love and support of all the Divine Mothers who are extensions of the one and only Divine Mother. It's a sign of how beautiful and grand she truly is and how important it is that we honor her day in and day out because without her love and nourishment, we wouldn't be able to grow, be, and create the way we do. She is the powerhouse, the lighthouse and ultimate garden, warrior, teacher, Mother, and everything in between. So embrace those growing pains and allow them to transform you. Know that they are a true sign that life isn't finished with you yet and that there is more Love, more joy, and more of you waiting to bless you on the other side.

God Fearing Woman.

God fearing woman how lambent is your soul.
You are the torch, the light bearer, and Star leading North.
God fearing woman you are justice and truth,
You refine through your love and uplift through your wisdom.
You empower through your prayer and awaken through your glory.
You are the land of Milk and Honey, where life and love go to flourish.
Peaches and cream, you don't aim just to please.
Sweet like passion fruit, birds and the bees.
Thick like caramel, like dinner is on me.
In me, come and eat, 'cause I got what you need.
As tender as a magnolia on a warm summer eve,
They fall to their knees to get a taste of your ecstasies.
God fearing woman you are grace, you are mercy.
For there is nothing more precious than the love of a woman,
that dances with the angels and sings words of luster.
She's all the 7 wonders breathing and in motion.
She teaches love, compassion, patience, and wonder.
Her cries spark revolutions and strikes like thunder.
Her hips write melodies and her heart tells the stories,
Of many cosmic mysteries, you'll believe God is a woman.
Her soul is tempered, yet wild, pure, and passionate.
For there is no greater love than from a god-fearing woman.
For there is no greater treasure than to feel in her pleasures.
Then to be replenished by her Sacred Love, Cosmic Waters, and

SEYLAH LOVE

Heavenly Sacraments.
Through her womb, she gives life and bears fruit upon the Earth,
That will sprout into nations, and kingdoms all over the world.
Blessed by God's hands, His Grace, and His Words,
By the blood of the covenant, sustained by the life of the Eternal.
God Bless the God-fearing woman for she holds the keys and has the
power,
To anchor heaven onto Earth and shatter all that is hell's desire.
For there is no jewel more precious than the love that she showers.
No mountain she cannot climb and no war she cannot battle.
No soul she cannot revive, no heart she cannot touch.
No life she cannot change and no mind she cannot grow.
For her voice resonates with the melody of Gaia's own heart,
432 Hertz, the sweetest song of all on Earth.
God-fearing women how precious you are to me.
How I will follow where you lead and sing songs of jubilee,
For how grateful I am to you, you god-fearing women.
I thank the earth, the stars, and heaven for the gift of you and your
presence.
For the rise and awakening of these goddesses embodied.
Oh how I love you and praise you, you god-fearing woman.
For you are a gift given, a miracle birthed,
From the heart and womb of the Holy Mother who is the creatrix of
all.

A Musing for the Muse.

What a gift it is to witness you.
What a gift it is to watch you embrace,
All the secrets, pleasure, and power in your divine and Holy breath.
What a gift it is to bear witness to your immanence.
To watch your heart dance in the fire of your internal sacraments and
holy relics.
Protected by the sacred temple that was blessed and created by the
most powerful of all artists.
You drip honey, grace, brown sugar, and all that is Great.
You brown coco goddess, how you are a sight for sore eyes.
The world shakes when you step,
And it sings as you walk with the mightiness of the Holy Mother's
luminescence.
The seas dance and the trees rejoice at the whisper of your name.
You holy woman.
You are wild with passion, hunger, and thirst,
For all things that mirror the same beauty and gold found within the
depths of your soul and heart.
What a gift it is to witness you.
What a gift it is to watch you embrace your own internal pleasures
hidden in the depths of your smile and gaze.
What a gift it is to see you dance in the discovery of Mona Lisa's
secrets.
You Holy woman.

SEYLAH LOVE

With grace, poise, and stature.
With lips that taste of fire, nectar, and Holy Love.
Ne Me Quitte Pas,
My sweet darling,
For I love you for life. Forever and always.

A Look Into Her Insides.

A beautiful mess made up of Florida water and incense smoke.
Made up of primordial blood and the hopes and prayers of her
ancestors.
Made up of cosmic whispers and ground-up stardust.
A walking contradiction who is only sure of the unsureness that
pushes and pulls the tides of her soul.
A dangerously inviting beauty full of fire, wrath, and no fucks.
What a great fuck—what a hypnotizing touch.
What a muse full of unbridled power, passion, and magick.
What a muse full of innocence with a never-ending inquisitiveness.
A beautiful mess made up of uncontrollable wonder and laughter.
Made up of "I dare yous" and tender submission.
Full of Milky Ways, dark seas, and mystical forests,
Full of songs oozing pleasure, hunger, and wild callings.
A beautiful mess made up of Florida water and Fire.
Whose halo is hidden behind brown eyes and a charming smile.

Sweet Spots (Foreplay with Life).

It's becoming increasingly clear to me that I reside in my own hidden
world.
A world where miracles happen every day and the fae come out to
dance in the twinkling sun of day.
Free, exposed, and full of blissful joy, I am the glory I've been
searching for.
I live on the intersection of heaven and earth.
That sacred crossroad,
That sweet spot—
Where they kissed and caressed until the Milky Way was born.
The Highway of the Gods and the Mysteries of Life.
Where the I Am resides and their whispers and melodies echo from
the total truth of their Womb and Mind.
I am enclosed in all of its beauty and wonder.
I smile and passionately play with the Muses under-covers,
As the muse that is my Life merges with me in a union bound by
unconditional love and sacred play.
Full of foreplay and ecstasy that makes my soul quake.
From the Divines Heart to mine, melodies for my whines.
I can't stop until it's done, that damn audacity of mine.
All these beautiful moments held in a capsule deep inside
I am proud to give purpose to this thing called Time.
I am proud to be One with the All, Everything, and Nothing at all.

SOMETIMES I LIE AWAKE AT NIGHT

Through my Breath, I give It form.
Through my Being, I give It matter.
Through my Life and Becoming I give it Purpose,
And Through my Love, I give it Existence.

Cosmic Musing #2

The Oracles
Genesis—The Void, the
Vessel & the Madness.

Sometimes I lie awake at night and the words won't slow and the thoughts won't stop. I do my best to express what it is that is tearing my mind into pieces—my heart bridled by the gunshots and wounds of yesterday. But there is healing. I do my best to anchor myself into the now and to only focus on what's in front of my face, but my heart and my soul are reaching for things that I cannot identify or obtain— my mind attempts to give life to the things of the dead in these winter times and cold night exchanges.

I feel like I'm losing, even though there is nothing to win. I feel like I'm stagnant, hungry for the beating of Life's existence. Stillness is my enemy— although the silence holds me in the places that the sun cannot reach. My spirit slows and it teaches me lessons that I've been running from, but my mind doesn't seem to get the message. It tortures me with what-ifs and dreams of betrayal ridden with paranoia and loneliness.

I'm here and then I'm not. I'm there and then I'm near. It's quiet and then it's chaos. War brewing deep inside driven by frustration and the madness of being alive. I try to contain it so it won't spill out and rot what's real even when it's not. We are all mad here, that's what the Hatter said, so I do my best dance with the demons in my head because they are the only ones who make me truly feel sane. They hold me close and remind me of Home and how even in the sun's glow I'll always live in between the gallows—between death and the horizons of life where the sea kisses the shore driven by the tides of the moon.

There is a place for darkness, there is a place for the haunted. There is a place in between being real and just a formless thought. There is a place for the dreamers who can't seem to tolerate the demands of the reality of Life. There is a place for those who'd rather find solace in the exile of their minds than live in the dread and despair that irks even the lightest of hearts and minds.

Tell me, sir, where do I go to live where the lights are on? Where do I go to live and dance in the seas where the dolphins sing and the mermaids lay blissfully in the breeze? Where my darkness can be loved just as much as the angels beside me and where people can recognize the unending sea in me without being terrified of drowning? Does a place even exist? Can it even be true? Is there a place where my broken wings can be loved just as much as my passionate heart yearns to? Is there even a space? Is there even a place? Is there even a way for the children of Osiris? Who live on the brink of death and chaos in every given blessed moment. Is there even a chance for the children of Oya? Who live on the middle path of everything and nothingness. Who's only a tear and temperament away from becoming hurricanes and lightning full of fury? Is there even love for the children of Durga, who live to be rebellion and fire? Who live to bear the weight of the universe while eating all the wicked and unrighteous. Is there even a place where the wild can be free without feeling damned and condemned? Without feeling alone, unwanted, and dangerous— All because we can dance with what makes others frigid? I didn't ask to mirror the depths of the endless or for it to be my salvation and Home. I didn't ask to harbor all of its secrets or to be birthed from the voids of the cosmos. I didn't ask to be a part of the wild and mysterious and of the things that make others flee. I didn't ask to be bred from primordial blood and to be born as a thing of urban legends. I didn't ask to be the thing connected to the things that few see and little live to tell. I didn't ask to share heart and soul with the Seven Sisters— to bear the weight and beauty of their heavenly existence.

But here I am. A black hole and supernova walking. Living, Breathing and Birthing— Creating, Destroying and Exposing. A physical manifestation of Mayu and the Void— dare I say it, that God is a Woman. Twins that mirror each other through infinite time and space, seeking cosmic and universal balance, harmony, and peace. This beautifully flawed human skin and physical existence created from their desire to experience on a tangible level—a cosmically fueled vessel meant to animate and give form to their breath and magic in motion. From their emergence and their womb was Creation and Existence birthed and given purpose.

Who is she? What is her story? Where is she really from? She is, I Am—We were, born from the womb of Order and Chaos, in the middle of Heaven and Earth—In the depths of the universe's heart and starry ocean. True Origins unknown to man—Only clear to the stars and the Originals who birthed them. Is she real? Is she human? What really is her soul? Only the Cosmos, I Am— She— will ever truly know. Mysteries only the Holy Mother and Father will ever fully know the depth of—Protected by the Bull and the cosmic Hunter, she holds the secrets of the Oracle. Is she good or bad? Is she devilish or holy? I Am, We are—She is neutrality, love, creation, beauty, and destruction. Our complexities are our superpower and the very essence of our being. I Am, She is— We, will always Be and have been since before the dawn of time you see.

You want to love me do you now? You want to know me you claim? You want to figure out all of the secrets hidden in the Mysteries within my veins. I bet you do. I bet you think you're well endowed enough to break and plow through my walls— To retrieve and receive all you are seeking, so you won't just feel like a fly lingering on the wall. Well, guess what dear one this is not a puzzle you wish to piece. Don't mistake this pretty face for a good night and easy street. She was birthed from the Sphinx, so if you do not have the keys, know you will get lost in the chambers of her Mysteries. Hungry, confused, and obsessed with her essence. If you don't have the knowledge, courage, and patience, don't dare try to walk and unlock her hidden labyrinth.

Don't let this pretty face fool you she is the Ethers embodied. There are sirens in her sea that will only once give a warning. A daughter birthed from the darkness, she thrives where the hounds run and the wolves play. She dances in the flames with a smile on her face—-initiated through the fire a million times, again and again. She charms the snakes that would otherwise eat and constrict others. They gather around her in deep devotion and wonder. With 4 heads she sees, feels, and understands deeply— her heart is as big as every planet put together please understand me. She dances with nymphs and sings songs with the fairies. She converses with the angels and plays tag in the heavens. She communes with the gods as an oracle she was birthed—known and respected in every dimension, plane, and galaxy. She's free. Loved, and hated by many. She is, We are, I Am— a beautiful embodiment of Love, Truth, and Creation. She is, We are, I Am— undefinable, unexplainable and unending. We are light, we are darkness, and everything in between— She is, We are, I Am.

The Inconceivable and Me.

Broken marble scattered all over the floor.
A tear-stained face looking for saving from the stars in heaven's grace.
A missing piece,
Something inside always feeling not quite fed or straight.
Not quite at peace or witnessed and appreciated in all of its existence.
A welcoming heart for the destructible.
A tender heart for the wear and tearable.
Frustration for what has grown unbearable and seemingly
unattainable...
The mundane seems to threaten everything magical in my mind.
In my spirit, where the magical is my lifeline.
Where the magical is the IV in my veins— the ventilator keeping my
body and brain alive and awake.
In my mind and the world we create,
Where the ravens sing songs of grace and the waterfalls only cry tears
of joy from a magnificent embrace,
Of all of the love, beauty, and passion riddled through the Earth's
ambiance and presence.
In my mind and the world we create,
Where the Earth is healthy and everything is simple and pure under
the eyes of the Divine's omnipresence.
Praying for more than understanding.
Searching for more than comfort and contentment.

SOMETIMES I LIE AWAKE AT NIGHT

Wishing and hoping that my surrender brings more than expected.
More than earned and deserving.
More than imagined and dreamed of.
The ruthless voices scream in my direction,
Telling me I am nothing but crazy and misguided.
That I am full of wishful thinking because it does not abide by what
my mind can define.
But my soul will not abandon all of the faith fairing in my spirit.
The knowing that crows louder than any of the denials I'm hearing.
Inside and out,
The faith that keeps my heart hopeful and believing.
That keeps the magic pumping fiercely throw my soul and my being.
That keeps me striving for all of the inconceivable things my mind
struggles to believe in.
Broken marble scattered all over the floor.
They glisten like diamonds in between the tears that fall.
Hope, despair, and destruction collide in the chambers within.
Wishing on a North Star that never seems to listen.
A frustration for what has grown unbearable and ill-fitting.
The mundane seems to threaten everything magical in my being.
In my mind and under those God-forsaken eyes...
Praying for more than comfort and contentment.
Wishing and hoping that my surrender brings more than expected.
More than conceivable and deserving.
More than imagined and dreamed of under God's divine mind.
Praying that what is missing becomes found.
That the pieces become fixed and the insatiable becomes as full as a
tick.
That the primal within finds resolution in its own being.
That I don't lose the human in me to the nature of the inconceivable...

Cosmic Musing #3:
Peace in my Humanity.

Sometimes I lie awake at night and struggle to bring peace and ease to the thoughts that only bring forth never-ending questions and emotional contortion. Sometimes I get so lost in trying to understand why I feel certain things that I wind up going into mad scientist mode and hitting the 13th floor. I obsess over understanding it all and then I become an exhausted puddle of thoughts, feelings, and anxieties. Sometimes I fall into feeling extremely incompetent when I can't solve or understand the questions and paradoxes that arise within my soul. Perhaps it stems from my desire to be so well versed in all there is to know about myself, God, and the world that I end up allowing my mind to collapse unto itself creating this internal black hole that consumes all of me. Maybe I am also haunted by the depths and parts of myself that I don't yet know, so much so that I pick myself apart and break myself down in attempts to stop it from driving me. I work so hard to grow and understand the makeup of my soul because the evolution of my spirit is so important to me but I've come to understand that the way to the answers and solace I seek don't come by way of force or the overworking of my mind but rather In me just being, observing and accepting. Accepting that I am limitless and complex and that I cannot figure out all of my soul in one-lifetime existence. Why if that were the case there would be no purpose for life itself and that would mean that God is more limited, definitive, and calculable than what we have been led to believe. But the existence of the universe, the soul, and all of creation itself shows that that could never be the case. Life and the human experience is an opportunity for us to meet ourselves and the Divine as deeply, tangibly, and consciously as possible over and over again until we figure out that anything outside of us is not the answer or solution. Until we figure out that Love, Life itself, Creation, and the Divine wanting to express themselves in infinite ways is the why, the reason, the answer, and the purpose.

Allowance, neutral observation, and acceptance are gateways to peace, flow, and enlightenment. Allowing yourself to feel it all. Allowing yourself to see God and be a perfectly imperfect part of the grand creation. Allowing yourself to not know. Allowing yourself to feel the tender, yet gritty feeling of being human and everything that it encompasses judgment-free. By accepting yourself, life, existence, and the infinite for all that it is and all that it is not— you will find everything you seek. Accepting that in order to live fully and freely, you have to make peace with being alive and that means learning to love and embrace the human condition from top to bottom. You have to make peace with your breath, your mind, your heart, and your soul. You have to accept and make peace with the fact that life is far more intricate and complex than we'd like it to be—-and by living as simply and open as we can, we can fall into a flow state that allows us to not feel so burdened, stressed, and overwhelmed by it. To embrace and accept our humanness as we allow and observe the mysteries and complexities of Life to continuously unfold around us judgment and attachment free is how we begin to embody true transcendence and peace. We go from unconscious fear-based living to conscious love-based living. It is how we step out of living in mad scientist mode and into hermit mode where serenity, harmony, and unity are readily available. Where pure insight and wisdom await to inform and teach us in every given moment. No force, mental burnout, or spiritual masochism needed, but rather searing presence, openness, and humility will do.

My Black Girl Needs.

Growing up I've always longed for a safe place.
A place where I could be seen, supported, and uplifted in all my
naturalness.
A place that accepted me for where I am now,
While motivating me on my journey to expand my heart and soul.
I searched high and low, in all four corners.
From the darkest of nights to the brightest of mornins'.
I looked for this place that I yearned for and longed.
I sought out a place where I didn't have to hide anymore.
A place where people would open their hearts to me and my love,
A place that didn't seek to change me, but accepted me flaws and all.
From an early age, they teach black girls that we are each other's
competition.
Silent ego wars and envy corrupt the budding before it can even begin.
They teach us to sabotage each other, judge each other, and condemn.
When all we need is each other's love, kindness, and tenderness.
Instead of holding space for each other, we try to take it away.
Sometimes we don't even notice the silent programming that makes us
behave this way.
That tells us if another black woman shines that we won't get our day,
But it's lies that have been ingrained in us from the day they locked
our ancestors away.
We've forgotten the power we hold as children of the sun.
As descendants from a black womb that birthed the nation.

SOMETIMES I LIE AWAKE AT NIGHT

We are mightier together when we move as one,
When we unify, recognize, and encourage the power that ripples in all
of us.
The world is already so cruel towards our melanated skin,
So why do we turn around and emanate that same insidious hatred?
We've forgotten how important and revolutionary sisterhood and
kindred-ship really is.
Let's open up the space for us to have these raw and vulnerable
conversations.
It hurts me to think about how I have always seen,
Black women at war with each other and never in a place of true
community.
It hurts to think about how I have never experienced,
Pure sisterhood in the presence of beautiful black women.
I've always been at the mercy of the latter I explained,
Where competition, judgment, and extreme individualism have
gotten in the way.
Where we struggle to uplift and empower each other in truth and
togetherness.
I seek to bring an end to this parasitic virus.
As black women, we are forced to grow up so quickly.
And we are immediately assigned the title of "strong black woman".
We are never extended the grace or space to feel and release,
or to seek refuge when we are burdened by the way a black woman
must move in society.
The way we have to be hyper-vigilant in the protection of our minds
and bodies,
In the protection of our voices, rights, our childhood, and innocence.
Where can we go for some protection, peace, and tenderness?
In a world that seeks to drown us in trauma, chaos, and violence.
As black women we hold so much magick in our souls,
We make the world go round and they don't want us to know.

That without black women the world would surely go cold,
As we are the bread, the butter, the blueprint, the backbone.
We make the world go round but they don't want us to know.
That's why they try to blind us from our beauty and the power we
hold.
That's why they deny us in public and then copy us from head to toe.
That's why they turn us against each other so we'll never know,
How powerful and important our presence truly is in this world.
There are so many black girls and women that search like me,
For community, family, support and somewhere to exercise their grief.
There are so many black girls and women that are just like me,
that want to have a sisterhood, a sacred space that allows them to just
be.
There are so many black girls and women who feel just like me,
who are hurt by the lack of togetherness and kinship, we crave more
unity.
There are so many black girls and women that long just like me,
for a place that will accept them and all their eccentricities.
There are so many black girls and women just like me,
who are tired of the competition and war, we should be each other's
peace.
For our sakes and the little black girls that look like you and me,
let's unplug from the conditionings that keep us separate and at arm's
length.
For our sakes and the little black girls that look like you and me,
let's give them the sacred space that we so desperately need and seek.
For our sakes and the little black girls that look like you and me,
let's bring back the sacredness of community and sisterhood again.
To the little black girls that look like you and me,
I promise to create a space that is made to embrace, uplift, and support
your black girl needs.

The Wailings of a Tender Heart.

Shallow breaths for deep wounds and deep wounds created by the coldness and aggression of man's madness manifested.
Shallow love creating disconnected people.
Disconnected people playing hot potato with empty words and trivial actions void of presence or any real sense of thoughtfulness and consideration.
Empty hearts. Empty love. Empty minds. Empty spirits.
Shallow breaths for deep wounds and deep wounds piercing the lungs of the victims of selfish love,
With nowhere to call a place for their bodies and hearts home.
Shallow love creating disconnected people. Disconnected people wandering around aimlessly, using the nearest heart not frostbitten as a charging station.
Using the nearest body as an object for all pleasure-seeking intents and purposes.
Using each other like toys and clothing.
Playing hot potato with empty words and trivial actions void of any true care, love, or nourishment.
Empty hearts. Empty love. Empty minds. Empty spirits.
I walk around screaming where is the love? Where is the motherfucking love?
I stomp and I wail in the name of Mary because I am tired and I am angry.

I see the people and their faces. I see the blood running through the
veins under their skin under the sun's luminescence.
I hear them inhaling and exhaling— all these visible signs of life,
But all I hear and feel are empty hearts, empty spirits, and empty
minds—with no movement or no love anywhere to be found.
The imitation of life— an illusion of love.
Their hearts are beating but there is no real life. There is no texture,
depth, or warmth in sight.
All I see is breath being used to curse thy neighbor.
Eyes cold and void —aching vessels running around spilling fractured
light force and poisoned blood all over the place, all over each other.
Blood all over the dance floor. Blood all over Gaia's body. Blood all
over the stained concrete where a child was just gunned down at the
4th of July block party.
Blood all over the school. Blood all over the home— where a
motherless child's tummy has been growling for days with no hope.
Where a mother screams as she's being thrown around by a father full
of malice and rage — who has bloodshed and violence on his agenda
every day.
Blood flowing all through the river. All in the soil.
There is blood everywhere, everywhere I turn.
My heart cries the holy mother and father weep because there is blood
everywhere.
Shallow breaths and deep wounds everywhere. Disconnected people,
empty hearts, twisted souls, and blood everywhere. I cry and I scream,
I shout out where is the Love?
Tears stream down my face as I am kicked down, judged, and
abandoned.
Tears stream down my face as I look for a shoulder to cry on but am
only met with glares full of disgust and disappointment.
Tears stream down my face as the homeless man on the corner is
kicked down, cursed at, and judged.

SOMETIMES I LIE AWAKE AT NIGHT

As my trans and queer family walk down the street in all of their glory— to only be met with glares of disgust, hatred, and acts of violence.
Tears stream down my face as the young black man gets beaten and abused by a system that wishes to see him lying cold and lifeless in the middle of the street.
Where is the love? Where the fuck is the compassion?
Where the fuck are the hearts that beat and the voices for those who are oppressed, alone, and meek?
Where is the hospitality, tenderness, and empathy? Where are the altruistic actions driven by the desire to just love, support, and honor one another? To love support and honor the God in all of us?
I ask as I wail.
As I walk through the valleys trying to find the answer as to why so many walk in this world so lonely with no home. With no love and no hope.
Why do so many walk this earth being victims of selfish love? Of greed, hatred, wickedness, and ignorance?
How did we get so disconnected?
How did we get so lost in our unified purpose?
To simply love, be, and exist in harmony with one another.
How come there are so many lone wolves with no tribe, no community, and no love for their nourishment?
What will it take to clean up and stop the running blood?
What will it take to put life and love back into our homes?
What will it take to put life and love back into the world?
How can we heal these shallow breaths, troubled hearts, and empty souls?
Because I'm tired of the cold.
Because I'm tired of having to step over all of this blood.

Let Love—.

Tell the truth and shame the motherfucking devil.
Tell the truth and let it release the shame bidding on behalf of the
brokenhearted.
Tell the truth and let love—-
Tell the truth and let love, my dearest darling.
Love is patient, love is kind and gentle.
It is not selfish, it is not rash—nor is it resentful.
Love regenerates, resurrects, and transforms.
It transcends all human limitations, expectations, and dimensions.
It is not home for just one, but for all who seek and receive it.
It does not judge or abandon, for it is always waiting with deep
tenderness and compassion.
It is loyal to all who are loyal to it and the truth as it will have it.
It is the greatest alchemist, teacher, doctor, and reverend.
So Preach to me Love, tell me all of your greatest stories —
Strum my pain with your song and fill my belly with your fever.
Touch my soul and whisper to me your most kept mysteries and
secrets—
Let me baptize myself in them and praise you with deep reverence.
For you are the divine in motion, glory given physical formation.
Tell the truth and let love set you free, shame the hatred, and let the
heart sing.
Let it mend the brokenhearted and multiply the glee in all hearts that
answer its plea.

SOMETIMES I LIE AWAKE AT NIGHT

Tell the truth and shame the motherfucking devil.
Tell the truth and release the shame bidding on behalf of the
brokenhearted.
Tell the truth and let love—-
Tell the truth and let love.

A Magnolias Interlude #2:

If Not to Live for Realness...

If not to live for realness then what is there to live for? If not to live for the touch and laughter of the ones we love, the golden sunsets that personify only a bit of the inconceivable beauty of our Creator, the rainy nights full of cozy blankets and jazz that chariots the immediate transcendence of one's heart and mind then what is there to live for? Is Life automatically full of meaning because it is or is Life gifted meaning through the act of our individual souls consciously dancing and loving on and through it? They say that nothing is real and that nothing matters but if that's the case then what is Life truly the expression and manifestation of? Because it isn't nothingness. If it were nothingness we would cease to exist because how can a Soul, something so infinite and powerful exist to do what it was created to do in a world of nothingness? The Soul is real. The energetic transmissions that our hearts and minds put forth to create tangible experiences and happenings are real. Life in and of itself is Real because contrary to popular belief we can touch. We can smell it. We can feel it and we can see it. Life interacts with both our spiritual and physical senses simultaneously. Life is real. So if Life is real and is a conscious force and expression on its own then how can nothing matter? How can our breath not matter? How can our love, dreams, feelings, and daily actions not matter? If they don't matter then why is the power of intention so important? If nothing is real and nothing matters then why is searing presence so transformative? Why then are we taught to be mindful when it comes to the way we maneuver throughout the world and how engage with ourselves, other people, and everything around us? Dare I say it is because Life is real. Because we are real and the way that we choose to show up in our day-to-day life matters not just within our worlds but in the collective consciousness that we are all a part of. Living and loving consciously comes with a deep level of awareness of the true spiritual responsibility that we have to each other and the world. That spiritual responsibility comes with the understanding that Life is real and the way that we engage with the Divine is real and that we have a duty to utilize this sacred relationship to help elevate and empower not only ourselves but also those with whom we share this planet with. No, we cannot fix the world as one, but if together we all embrace the responsibility to live and love as consciously and intentionally as we possibly can then together we indeed can shift, shake, and change the world. The waves and tides of the ocean do not move or create currents as one but as a unified whole. They push and pull with the help of the moon's searing presence, support, and gravitational pull. In the same way, the divine helps push and pull us through their sacred song that our souls can hear and sense. The ultra-sound that is always playing and being sung by the guardians of heaven is constantly pulling us towards them and connecting us to the Most High. That is real. That presence is real. That energy is real so...

If not to live for realness then what is there to live for? Is Life automatically full of meaning because it is or is Life gifted meaning through the act of our individual souls consciously dancing and loving on and through it? They say that nothing is real and that nothing really matters but if that's the case then what is Life truly the expression and manifestation of? Because how can a Soul, something so infinite and powerful exist to do what it was created to do in a world of nothingness...

Cosmic Musing #4:
Universal Symphony and the Pulse of Life.

Sometimes I lie awake at night and think about how small I am in the grand scheme of things. One tiny, lone water droplet in a deep unending sea. Sometimes it makes me feel as if my life is unnecessary and unimportant. As if my tiny little existence means nothing in such a big world full of others. But then my soul reminds me of how one small water droplet helps make the big, bountiful sea the force that it is. Without that one singular droplet, an important piece that makes up the whole would indeed be missing. A Small but grand contribution made by millions of singular droplets unified together is what makes the ocean what it is. Without each other the sea becomes nothing. It simply could not exist. Therefore each soul, each droplet, is a vital part of the whole. No one is insignificant and each life is full of purpose and importance. We all play a role and we all possess unique potentials that contribute to the essence of the universal life force that pulsates through the existence of everything. We are all living as a unique One amongst other unique Ones, engaging in a universal symphony that's orchestrated and composed by our individual breaths, signatures, and expressions. I can't help but to be filled with so much pride and humility in understanding how essential my, and everyone's soul is to God, myself, and Life. I shutter in chills understanding how profound God's artistry and craftsmanship really is. For them to not only make the world as lively and intricate as it is, but to then very intimately create billions of specially designed souls who all have their own unique purpose, magic, medicine, and genius is utterly mind-blowing. The magnificence and beauty of it ALL is something that will always keep me moving and inspired. To know there is only One Me and one You in a sea full of divine creations is just mind-blowingly insane in the best of ways. I will always be filled with deep awe and amazement at the beauty of it all. I am so grateful for and appreciative of the variety of souls in this world because without them the picture could never make sense. The sea could never be and the song could never played. I am very inspired and humbled by their greatness and grand being alike. The more I bear witness to my breath and observe as I instinctively anchor the divinity in me into the world through my expressions, the more eager I am to bear witness to others doing the same. All different kinds of tunes of love and creation playing, vibrating, and dancing together to form the rhythmic beat of the Divine's Heart. The Pulse of Life. A universal orchestra that we all play a chord in and are a vital part of. There is truly nothing else in this world like it and I'm so grateful to be alive and a part of it. To belong to something so exceptional. To play with and be connected to such extraordinary souls. I don't think there is an honor in the world that could ever supersede this one and it's one I'll always be the proudest of. And in those moments I begin to question my purpose or importance or feel I'm losing sight of myself and what truly matters, I'll come back to this. And I'll allow myself to be reinvigorated and humbled by the love and power of the Divine and Universal Symphony again.

An Ode to Love.

I love. I love. I love.
I love until it consumes me and demands I transform to meet it at new
levels within its Mysteries.
I oblige with glee, when it demands I go further into my seas to
become more pure and holy in all of its glory.
What happens when love becomes the one you cannot live without?
When it feels like it sustains your soul the way your breath and body
does?
When passion and pleasure become the only language you know how
to speak?
What happens when love becomes the honey and you the bee?
In a world full of war, hatred, and greed— how does one learn to safely
be what love wants us to be?
Where does one go for beauty and sweets?
Anywhere and everywhere— love is omnipresent you see.
Just look with eyes wide open, through the eyes of your inner child
you'll see.
My soul suckles at the breast of the everlasting bliss and truth that love
provides for me.
In all of its different homes, gardens, laughs, and heartbeats.
It is love that I find even in the cracks of the concrete,
full of roses and sunflowers parading as miracles in their simplicity.
I look for it in her smile, her womb, her heart, and how pleased she is
with me.

SEYLAH LOVE

I look for it in the skies, in the music, and my body as it sways to the
beat.
I never have to look too hard for She is always just inches away you see.
What happens when love becomes your greatest lover you ask me?
Why you see God in all things near, dear, and yonder.

The Power of the Dreamers.

Here is to keeping Hope alive.
Here is to being the most powerful thing in the world: A Dreamer.
A soul rooted in Hope, Faith, and Trust.
In a vision not yet manifested and a sight not often understood.
Here is to being a Dreamer. A soul who crafts wonder into the world.
A beacon of light in all the darkness and a magician whose creations
are their sword.
Out of their Hope magick is bred and miracles are quickly born.
Out of their Creations Beauty is shared and souls are sparked and
transformed.
Here is to keeping Hope alive.
Because when the world turns grey and your dreams decay,
where else do you go to raise the dead?
Our inner child's greatest weapon and healing medicine.
The thing that keeps us afloat in a world full of sorrow and disarray.
Without Hope, there is no Dreaming and without dreaming we
become lost.
We become stuck in perpetual cycles of darkness, where there is no
light or growth.
We become angry, jaded, and bitter, closed off to the Beauty of the
world.
To the Beauty and Wonder in each other and our potential to change
the globe.

91

Out of Hope magick is quickly born, fueled by our innocence and inner child's love,
And that's why we must remain vigilant in protecting it in each other because no matter what we all deserve Wonder.
So here is to being a Dreamer.
A soul who weaves Hope into the world.
A beacon of light in all the darkness and a magician whose creations are their sword,
So Magick, Love, and Glamour are not lost in the grayness of the world.

Cosmic Musing #5:

Language is Limiting. Interconnectedness, Deep Feeling & Art Precedes It.

Sometimes I lie awake at night and think about how at moments I just do not have the words to clearly articulate the things I am feeling and experiencing. I think about how difficult and almost seemingly impossible it feels sometimes to give physical form to things so abstract and complex like thoughts, emotions, and other deeply internal experiences. As humans, we genuinely just want to feel seen, heard, understood, and validated. Sharing our emotions, thoughts, and experiences with others is how we attempt to connect and bond. Feeling like we do not have the proper ability to give life to the thoughts, feelings, and mysteries inside of us clearly and concisely, can often make us feel alone and misunderstood. I feel that a part of the issue is language in and of itself. Human language is beautiful, yes, but I feel like it is also extremely limiting and confining. With that being said, however, I do understand that it is the main way that we have to communicate given the level that we are at collectively in human evolution. It's not that we are yearning to express things that cannot be clearly expressed or understood, it's just that we have become stunted and limited in our ability to do so because of how distanced and disconnected we have become. We have become increasingly blind to the fact that we are all interconnected and that we are all one big soul family that are colorful extensions of the universe and the Most High. We are extremely disconnected from one another's hearts and souls and we no longer feel each other with deep intensity and sensitivity the way that we used to. Once upon a time, we were able to feel, see, and converse with one another without the need for words or games because we were all consciously tapped into the universal One and Mind. We just felt and understood each other through the invisible energetic roots that connect us all and through them, we had a direct connection to each other, Gaias, the Divine themselves and damn near everything in Creation's thoughts, feelings, and experiences. We saw each other because we clearly felt each other. No extras in between. Just pure, unfiltered openness and connectedness. Language wasn't needed. It was an unnecessary barrier and I think oftentimes that's why I feel I've struggled bonding with people because they just do not feel me. And if they cannot feel me, it makes it very difficult for them to see me, so I've often wandered Earth feeling very alone and out of place. Our languages and resonances are different both physically and spiritually and no matter how hard I try to speak from my heart, I often wind up feeling like an alien still. Literally and figuratively. Initially, I used to think something was wrong with me and that I was difficult and an absolute weirdo. I used to think people would purposefully misunderstand and misperceive me until I realized a heart cannot clearly understand and see something if it's disconnected and speaking in an energetic frequency that's vibrating on a completely different field than the other heart. It's not being done on purpose, it's just that they simply cannot hear or see you because they cannot feel you. The roots that connect us all have been clogged and twisted and our hearts aren't as open, some not at all, due to personal and societal traumas, barriers, and distortions. The more that we heal and open our hearts on an individual level, the more we can see, feel, hear, and connect on both a personal and spiritual level. Where words will then take a back seat to the impactful embrace of Feeling. Feeling doesn't require physical touch or sight the way we think it does. Just a clear, open, and receptive heart, soul, and activated higher mind. We have hundreds of invisible sensory receptor points in and around our energetic and etheric fields that allow us to be able to tune into and receive signals and information directly from everything around us. Deep feeling requires total presence and surrender to the now and when we embrace our sensitivities and fully tune into our energetic sensory system, we can see and perceive clearer and sharper than our physical eyes ever could and understand things our physical mind could not even comprehend. The mind likes to distort and strip down but the heart likes to experience, understand, and digest the whole of something as purely and true as possible. So when we embrace presence and deep feeling, we allow our hearts to do that all the time, at any given moment. We are then able to form clear and direct pathways, connections, and relationships to everything around us, which allows us to see, feel, and experience all things in a deeply meaningful, profound, and euphoric way.

Language can be very limiting and we've come to understand that as humans and that's the main reason we've created so many different types of mediums to try to give voice to the space in between words, the thoughts in our thoughts, and the depth of the things that we feel but have no idea how to explain. Music, poetry, singing, painting, and dancing et., all of these things are tools we use to help the the heart and soul feel seen, understood, and heard. We use them to try to explain and express what the naked mind cannot understand but what the soul can. We use it to give life to the things in our hearts that language sometimes just cannot adequately capture. Art is how we transcend the Earthly and allow our souls to have direct contact, communication, and connection with each other and the All that's in between. Art is divine communion and a sacred conversation between Source, the artist, and the soul witnessing and experiencing it. It's intimate, raw, and straight to the Heart. There is no space for confusion or misunderstandings.

Just clear, unfiltered conversation being had and sacred space being shared and that's why so many create— To bypass the limitations of the mind and the Earth we live in that often distort and negatively filter the messages, codes, and truths of our hearts and who we are in our souls. Art breaks down that space and speaks directly to our entire being in a way that language just cannot do a lot of the time. I feel human language doesn't do the soul justice and I will forever feel that way. When the language we physically speak just will not capture and transmit accordingly, that's when we turn to Art In hopes that if we turn to the right dial on the station, maybe just maybe someone will hear, see, and understand us loud and clear.

A Magnolias Interlude #3:

The Gift of Searing Presence and the Seasons of our Life.

Practicing searing presence within our lives helps us to see and understand that there is always something valuable and beautiful for us to capture and feel within each moment that we are here. Searing presence helps us to view things with objectivity and neutrality, allowing us to take in things more rawly. It supports us in seeing things more purely, closer to the essence of what it is, and not for what our preconceived notions, projections, triggers, or ego try to get us to see. It allows us to see, sense, and filter our experiences more so throughout our heart space and Spirit and not just through our minds. This opens us up more to The Divine, truth, universal knowing, wisdom, and understanding. We become more spiritually astute.

Each season and cycle within our lives is important, even if we can't always see how or why in the moment. They each hold a range of experiences, all of which are meant to teach us and help us evolve and expand on all levels. Mama Gaia has her seasons, and we watch her cycle through them again, and again and again as we live out our lives here on her soil. We, as her children, emulate and mirror her through the act of having our own important physical and spiritual seasons. These seasons hold a sort of "spiritual lesson plan" meant to help with our evolution and development on all levels. That spiritual lesson plan is like a syllabus for our Spirit, containing all of the things we will be working on that will help us learn, grow, heal, and transform physically and spiritually. All of this physically manifests as the Art of Experience; or Life itself. This is what makes us Alive. We experience the Divine themselves in everything and they teach us about Love, Truth and All That Is through the "classes" we take in each season and cycle. As we live and work through these classes, we are meant to grow and expand and then share all we've gathered with others. This is how all of Life and Spirit work to support us all. Each season and cycle prepares us for the next in some way shape or form. Sometimes this looks like spirit making you take a job that is far out of your comfort zone, and you not knowing this job is just preparation for something better than you could have ever imagined. Not knowing this job is giving you tools and knowledge that will help you excel even more in your next endeavor. Not knowing that this job is helping you master discernment and setting boundaries. Not knowing that the job is helping you heal inner child wounds and help you better understand how to care for yourself. Sometimes spirit puts us in certain places for however long we may need, to learn something or gain the physical or spiritual resources and know how that we may need, that will help us in the next level. We may see a slow season and begin to think we may be doing something wrong or that something bad is happening, not understanding spirit is giving us the space and time to rest and rejuvenate after all of our hard work. Sometimes we have to slow down and go into hermit mode so that we can go within to integrate and embody the knowledge and insights we need for the next season of our lives. Sometimes we need to go within to fine-tune some things, release some things, or further master some things before we are fully prepared for whats next. Every season serves a purpose and Spirit and Life itself are always actively helping us build and grow ourselves. We just have to be willing to follow their lead and remain patient, open, and present in each moment. Spirit and all of our support are always conspiring in our favor. Just because we may not understand the full reason for the season or see its piece in the whole puzzle immediately, it doesn't mean that it is not important or doesn't have a place. When we are present and accepting of where we are in each moment, we can begin to see the reasons naturally. And even in the moments where things are blurry or unclear, our faith in the Divine and trust in the universal truth that Life is always conspiring in our favor will carry us through. Our unconditional trust and faith will support us in our leaps and in the cycles and seasons where our clarity and insight become more lean and scarce. In those seasons where we have to truly be led by faith and not by sight.

When we become more present, open, and receptive to the divine intelligence that communicates with, teaches, guides, and supports us through every day, the more we can grow and live a full, well rounded life. We can utilize our gems of wisdom, knowledge, and spiritual/emotional intelligence with a greater sense of skill. We become better equipped on all levels, which supports us in becoming more self-empowered and actualized. Presence opens the door for us to move more fully and organically in empowered service, helping us to fulfill our divine mission and destiny accordingly. To me, this is what it means to be a conscious, sovereign being. This is what it means to be an alchemist and magician. It's wielding one's immediate physical and spiritual resources (wisdom, truth, awareness, faith, imagination, understanding, will, etc) to heal, transform, and nurture one's Life and soul as the cycles and phases come. It's using the magick within to master the Self, our experiences, and Life through the act of being present and conscious of Life and our experiences themselves. To be searingly present is to become the master of your Life.

A Magnolias Interlude #4:

The Subconscious Holds the Keys.

As we walk and travel along our healing, enlightenment, and personal development journeys, we often encounter many things that are very new and unfamiliar to our senses and souls. We will come across roads, experiences, and situations that will challenge and inspire us and that will help us grow on different levels internally and externally. These things often ask and sometimes force us, to flex and stretch the whole of our brains while allowing it to also look to and lean on the genius that is our spirit. The things our brain cannot process and understand on its own are the things we must allow our spirit to take hold of so that it may decipher and decode them in a way that provides total comprehension. Even if there are no words and just a full mind-body knowing and understanding through subtle soul-heart-to-subconscious integration. The subconscious mind is one of the most complex components we have within our being but it is also one of the most powerful tools that we possess and I feel that it continuously gets a bad rep along with its right-hand man: the Shadow. Some people look at the shadow and subconscious as one entity but I see them as two separate counterparts who work together. Just as the conscious mind is often associated with the light body or our higher selves, I associate the subconscious with our shadow and our primal selves. I believe that you cannot have a healthy, equally yoked relationship with Self and total mind, body, and spirit synergy if you only honor one part of yourself while neglecting the other. So many people take the initiative to run and venerate their higher selves while running away from, demonizing, and neglecting their shadow selves as if the shadow holds no importance at all. What I think people often do not realize is that your shadow self and subconscious can teach you a great deal about yourself and your internal structures and workings. Together they act as both an internal and external supporting tools that can help you have positive forward movement and progression within your healing, enlightenment, and personal development journeys, just like the way our higher self can. Our shadow and higher self share a very important purpose, which is to help us become the highest and most embodied version of ourselves. The differences between them are that they reside in different places within us and they go about helping us grow, heal, and develop in different ways. We have to be willing to understand and get familiar with how they operate within us individually first so that we can then learn how to balance them and use them together effectively and efficiently.

Our subconscious is the moon within us. It holds and guides the primal being and aspect of us that is wild, animalistic, and raw. The part of us that houses the dark feminine and/or masculine qualities we hold and where our instinctual impulses are rooted and expressed. Just like mother nature is heavily influenced by the moon and its energy, we as humans are also heavily influenced and driven by our internal subconscious moon. The subconscious motivates and drives our organic nature and way of being and that is why it is so important that we build a relationship with our shadow so that through it, we can gain a better understanding of how our mind works, what lies within the depths of it and how those things affect and manifest through us in our day to day. When given the opportunity, the shadow can shine a light on faulty perspectives, beliefs, conditionings, and programs that are holding us back from living, growing, and healing and that are creating self-induced states of suffering, chaos, and conflict. Whether imposed onto us by our environments, culture, familial influences and expectations etc., or internalized by us due to traumas and/or negative experiences, our shadow, and subconscious can give us the necessary tools we need to deprogram them so we can then download and integrate new software that will have a more positive and beneficial impact on our overall well-being, sustenance, and development. Our subconscious will then be constructed in a way where it naturally and automatically works in alignment with us and not against us. It will no longer influence us to build, live, and behave in ways that are a reflection of external inputs, factors, and trauma, but in a way that is reflective of our true internal makeup— supporting us in building and living genuinely authentic, fulfilling, nourishing, and supportive lives.

The shadow and subconscious can help lead you back to the parts of yourself that hold some of your most potent energy, power, and magic. It can help you reach a place of true self-actualization by teaching you how to have a more harmonious and disciplined relationship with the primal parts of you. The shadow helps us navigate through the trenches and valleys so that we can retrieve, restore, and reintegrate the parts of us that have been silenced, locked away, forgotten, or stuck in loops of trauma and pain. Your shadow wants to help you reclaim what was lost, taken, or fractured and help you put it back together again so that you can become more full and embodied. So that you can grow and move in the world with a greater sense of Self, power, confidence, sovereignty, and authority. Your shadow is not a demon. It is not here to torture you, or destroy you. It is here to help you find the keys and pieces that you need to revive and regenerate the whole of you so that you can achieve full spectrum healing and integration between the different dualities within you.

So many of us were taught to be afraid of our shadows before we even knew what they were and as we grew into adults it became second nature to ignore and hide from them. As children, we are taught that shadows are not safe or that they are mischievous hindrances like the way Peter Pan's shadow was. We are programmed to believe that what lies in the shadow(s) are bad monsters, forbidden things, or even worse — the dangerous unknown. As we were being taught this, we were subconsciously being encouraged and conditioned to reject certain parts of ourselves because they weren't all full of light, rainbows, and gumdrops. Everybody has a shadow or aspects of themselves that are darker and as humans, we must hold space for ourselves to feel and understand the full spectrum of what arises within. Heavier or shadowy emotions are not innately bad or harmful and it is only natural to experience them through life because not every day is smooth, bright, and perfect. As a collective, we are learning that not only is that an unrealistic and impractical way of living, but it is also extremely unhealthy to only focus on and embrace the positive or light parts of you. It can be psychologically, spiritually, and physically harmful to suppress your heavier or darker emotions in an attempt to bypass your way through life. Another thing that we learn early on that influences us to hide and run away from our shadow and even our heavier emotions is the notion that everything dark or shadowy is evil and that is just simply not true. There is a DISTINCT and huge difference between something being dark and something being evil. Everything that glitters and is light isn't gold and everything dark or shadowy isn't evil. Dark does not automatically equate to evilness and not everything evil is shrouded in darkness. Having a strong sense of discernment and a clear understanding of the qualities and functions of both can help one understand when something falls under either category. Darkness or in this case, our shadow is not inherently bad or harmful. In fact, they tend to operate from a more neutral place and are often very sensual and playful. What can make the shadow a bit scary or overwhelming is when it is constantly being influenced by unchecked fear, anger, anxiety, etc., and unattended to trauma and pain. The way it behaves when being overwhelmed by these things is what often gives the shadow a bad rep and I believe this is what leads to the creation of what we like to call inner demons. Inner demons are the energetic and emotional manifestations of the wounds and traumas within that have grown too big for our minds, hearts, and souls to hold and contain. The more we suppress and push our traumas and pains deep within our subconscious, the more our shadow stretches and grows to try to accommodate. The thing is though, there is only so much that it can hold and when it reaches its limit it fractures and breaks into multiple pieces. So instead of there being one whole shadow that is in line and trying to work with us, there then becomes multiple wild and uncontrolled mini shadows or " inner demons" that begin to wreak havoc, chaos, and turmoil over us. Instead of one whisper under the moon, it then becomes multiple loud voices and overwhelming energies. All of them screaming and raging trying to get our attention as they pull the mind, body, and spirit in every which way searching for something to fix them and put them back together again. We no longer are being influenced by one shadow, but rather multiple unruly ones, and because they are all mini containers holding our traumas, pains, and negative experiences, they do the only thing they know how to do to be fixed and recognized— physically recreate and manifest whatever traumatic energetic imprint they hold. They influence us to date certain people with who we can recreate that unhealthy relationship dynamic we had with our mother, father, or previous partner. They influence us to mentally sabotage or run away from the things that sustain us and make us happy because as children people constantly told us we weren't deserving. They influence us to physically and emotionally self-neglect and abandon because of the way others withheld their presence, love, and care from us. *TRIGGER WARNING* They influence us to behave hyper-sexually because of the sexual traumas and abuse that we were never able to address and work through. These energetic fragments can physically manifest in our lives in a multitude of ways and they can quite literally keep us stuck in the past because the pieces of our shadows and souls become frozen in those moments in time when the harmful experience occurred. We then can become emotionally, mentally, and spiritually stunted in our present day-to-day because those parts of ourselves are not able to grow, move, and progress in the ways they need, that is until we go through the process of soul retrieval through intensive 1-1 shadow work.

This is why shadow work is so important because it is the process of going within and sometimes even back in time to retrieve those pieces of us so that we can bring them back home, love on them, and mend them back into our souls. Shadow work is the process of going deep within the depths of our heart and mind so that we can put the fragments of our subconscious back together as we allow our shadow to help us revive and reintegrate the parts of us that were in a sense energetically and spiritually dead or disempowered. Shadow work is about reclaiming your time, life, energy, and power back as you call all parts of you home in the name of Love, truth, justice, and righteousness. It's the process of liberating and freeing yourself internally and externally so that you can walk this earth as the sovereign, autonomous, and divine being you were born to be. At any given moment, no matter how many times or how long it takes you can call all of those parts of you back home. You can reclaim all of your power back from those harmful people, things, and/or experiences. You can retrieve those parts of your soul and bring healing to their pains as you take the time to listen to them and give them a space to wail, shout, and rage. You can put the pieces back together so that you can grow, develop, and expand the way that you want, need, and desire too. You can obtain peace of mind. You can mend those pieces of your heart and soul so that you can come back into total fullness, wholeness, and unity within Self. It is never too late to start the healing journey and it is never too late to embrace working with your shadow and subconscious. Healing, obtaining peace, and becoming the most authentic, healthiest, and happiest version of yourself is possible. It is not a privilege allowed just for some rather it is a birthright for all. We all have the right to pursue and have joy, to live a life full of harmony and grace as we embrace our truth and purpose. This is what we are all here to do and working with our subconscious and shadow can help give us the keys, power, courage, and strength to do so.

It's true, that our pain only belongs to us, but if we embrace the alchemist within, we can turn that pain into something that can help, inspire, and support other people as they walk along their healing journeys. No one was meant to carry and work through everything alone and that's why it is so important that we give ourselves permission to share and speak out but also permit ourselves to seek help and support outside of ourselves. Yes, we must learn how to show up for and nurture ourselves, but I am a firm believer that the love of a friend and/ or community unit provides some of the most powerful medicine that could ever be given. We do not have to travel this journey of healing alone and we do not have to fix it all ourselves. Sometimes there are things we are not able to give to ourselves but our support system can give them to us in mounds. There is no shame in accepting help whether it's through another person or even prescription medication. Healing looks different for everyone and everyone will require unique methods of treatment and support because no two wounds, souls or life experiences are or manifest the same. It's so important that we focus on our own needs and experiences so that we can seek out the path and help that is most supportive for us. Healing is truly a journey and it is so very important that we extend ourselves grace and patience as we work on ourselves and move through life. No one on this planet is perfect and there will be times we fall short, take a misstep, and have days where we just simply cannot — and that is okay. Healing, mending your heart, and retrieving and restoring parts of your shadow, mind, and soul is not something that can happen overnight. Hell, it's not even something that can happen over days or a couple of weeks. Healing and shadow work require lots of time, energy, diligence, and patience as we do the work and build our spiritual, mental, and emotional resolve and aptitude along the way. As we take each fragment and each wound baby step by baby step, one day and a sea of tears at a time. But most importantly we must remember it is possible. That we will and can make it through. That we are deserving of peace, happiness, and joy. We are more than capable of showing up for and supporting ourselves as we allow others to show up for and support us along the way too. We must remember that it is a process and that Rome was not built in a day. Even on the days when it feels like the London bridge is falling, we must remember that we can always get to the other side because we have the bricks, the gaul, and the nerve to fucking do it—even if we have to take another way or build another fucking bridge. We must never give up on ourselves because we deserve Life. We deserve so much fucking Life and to have every ounce of joy and bliss that we desire. So don't be afraid to listen to your shadow or allow it to guide you to the parts of you that need the most love, tenderness, and care because as scary as it may initially seem, know it will only open up more avenues for love, peace, and healing in your life. Know and trust that you are always protected as you go within the chambers of your heart to be the balm of healing and relief that your mind, body, and soul need. Even if you have to do it a bit shaky, believe that you do have the power to be the divine physician you've always needed. It is in you and the Divine is assisting and supporting you every step of the way. So the next time you hear your shadow call your name, fragmented or not, stand tall and stand strong. Reach your hand out and dare to go within to bring more of you back home and back into you.

Cosmic Musing #6:

The Medicine that is Pleasure and the Catalyst that is Pain.

Sometimes I lie awake at night and think of how my life has taught me so much about pain and pleasure. I used to abuse each primary and it took me a long time to learn how to honor and appropriately use the medicine that the two provide. I believe that they are two sides of the same coin and as humans, we have a tendency to live our lives running from the pain while overindulging in the pleasure. But just as pleasure is a sure thing so is pain. We cannot run or hide from either. If we are willing to tolerate pain for physical beauty, why can't we tolerate temporary pain for the overall healing, growth, and beauty that it can bring to our souls? Pain isn't something that we can outrun or completely erase from our lives and pleasure isn't something that we can be engulfed in every second of everyday. Moderation is key and it is very important for our spiritual and physical wellbeing on all levels that we learn how to develop a healthy relationship with both. It's important that we learn how to use pleasure as a tool to help bring an aura of ease to the difficult moments we face in life and how to use pain to help guide us in our healing, toward empowerment, expansion and peace.

Pleasure helps us temper the pain we feel so that we do not get consumed and overridden by it. It helps us grow our tolerance and capacity for discomfort and widen our overall threshold for pain. Pleasure and beauty are life giving properties and they bring deep nourishment and vitality to our lives and souls. They remind us like that life is worth living and that we are truly not just here to suffer. Pleasure and intimacy are often reduced to just things we experience during sex, but the truth is they are so much more than that. They stretch so much further than that. Both can be brought forth and experienced in many different ways. Whenever we do things passionately, tenderly, thoughtfully, and intentionally with all of our being— we are being intimate with that experience and/or engagement which allows pleasure, beauty and joy to become the core and outcome of the exchange. When we sip our wine real slow and really savor the depth and complexity of the notes. When we slow dance with a beloved friend or partner and immerse ourselves in the aura of warmth, love and connection. When we laugh with all of our might and feel into our belly shakes and out coming waves of joy. When we sit outside alone. Deeply engaged with the world around us as we watch the birds fly and the clouds dance across the sky. In those moments we are being intimate with Life, ourselves and all that make up that engagement and experience. We are allowing ourselves to be immersed in and revitalized by the sweetness of pleasure and we can do so whenever we choose. Pleasure is everywhere because life itself is inherently erotic in nature but in order to witness and experience it fully, you have to be willing to embody searing presence. This requires vulnerability and transparency within your mind, body and spirit. You have to accept the invitation to be intimate with all that is beyond just your physical senses. This allows the soul to open wide so that it can experience the subtle waves of beauty, sensuality and pleasure that dance in the air around us at all times, generously and responsibly. Pleasure reminds us that pain is truly temporary and that we do not have to become or over identify with it. It also reminds us that one of our greatest gifts is the ability to feel deeply and that without that life would be dull, boring and meaningless. It reminds us of the power of our own beauty and sacred sexuality and that at any given moment we have the to ability to be immersed in a bliss of our own mental, spiritual and emotional making. No matter if we are alone, surrounded by the mundane or in deep pain. We have the power and ability as sensual and sexual beings to call forth the medicine of pleasure and use it to help heal, restore and soothe our souls in trying and painful times. Or in times where we just simply want to feel good and enthralled with life but again modern is key. Just like you can get lost in pain you can surly get lost in pleasure and going to far out in either can have unfavorable outcomes both physically and spiritually.

Pain is one of the greatest catalysts for change and disillusionment. It's extremely sobering and it grounds us, forcing us to come back down to earth so that we can face ourselves, our aches, and truth head on with fierce determination and resolve. It helps us to see our reality in the clearest manner possible, bringing us to the precipice of transformative insights and revelations about what is going on around and within us. It's when we begin to allow ourselves to see our pains more clearly, that we grow in our understanding of how to heal them, how to better show up for ourselves, and how to stop the ways we may be playing a role in our own suffering. Honest self-reflection and having the courage to sit and observe our aches help us understand how we can alchemize them and turn them into medicine, wisdom, power and beauty. It's important we do not dissociate or delude ourselves out of it, but rather learn how to navigate it with healthy detachment, tactful observation, and compassion so that we can heal it from the root up and not just halfway.

Transcending our suffering does not mean that we will never feel pain or that life will be rainbows and butterflies every day. It means that we have figured out how to not allow pain to drag us down to the pits of hell. It means we've figured out how to use it as a divine catalyst for healing, freedom, liberation, and peace. It's to understand that the key to wellness and transformation is not running away from the pain or discomfort but rather conversing with it and holding space for it. In order to transmute our pain into pleasure and beauty, we have to be willing to surrender to it. We have to be willing to hold our hurts and cry with them. We have to be willing to embrace them with deep tenderness and as they are often parts of ourselves in need of deep love and attention. We have to be willing to welcome them back home so they can feel empowered enough to become one with the light again. But without pain, we wouldn't be able to identify or find our wounds. We wouldn't be able to know what they need to feel loved, seen and heard. We wouldn't know that anything was wrong in the first place. When we allow pain to act as a guide and trust in our abilities as divine physicians we can turn even the most deepest of wounds into soul food and medicine. It is in times of pain that we must actively seek out pleasure and embrace the medicine it holds. It can be difficult to do so when all you feel is heaviness, but it is in those moments where we must fight our hardest to cultivate some sense of feel good or else we risk being swallowed by it all. Once you open up the space and invite even the smallest inkling of pleasure in, it will take root and expand naturally if you let it. Both pain and pleasure have a genius of their own and when we allow pleasure in, it will do what it was made to do with no needed efforts of your own. But the key is to get out of its way and let it work it's magic over your spirit in the way it knows you need.

I feel like a lot of the times when we are hurting we get so blinded by the whys and get so lost in trying to make it stop, that we don't see or recognize the amazing ability we hold as powerful beings to turn coal into diamonds and pain into pleasure and healing. We underestimate the power and force within and get lost in the voices that tell us we must run away from the pain. Our bodies may feel like they cannot bear the weight of feeling the pain, so out of fear and lack of trust in our abilities to swim and not sink, we do our best to suppress it through any means necessary. Our unchecked or unbalanced ego/shadow will try to convince us that if we don't run or if we don't hide that the pain will last forever. Those negative voices will try to blind us with false stories saying that we are not strong enough and that if we bend we will surely break. They'll tell us to give in and give up. But then we'll hear a little tiny voice saying no. We'll feel a tug within and feel our higher selves grabbing us by our arms, begging us to stand up and get on our feet. We'll feel our inner child begging for us to fight with them and we will feel our ancestors gathering around us rooting us on, giving us an extra dose of their love and support. We'll feel Spirit move within us, reminding us that we are loved and reminding us that the battle is not ours alone. In those moments the Divine asks us to let them in. To choose them and let them move and do the heavy lifting. A gentle reminder to those reading that no wound or pain cannot be healed or touched by the supreme love, power, and might of the Divine. But we must choose to fight for ourselves, our peace, and our joy no matter what force dares to shatter that or break us. We must remember that through the love of spirit, we will always be protected and fortified. So even when we feel weak, we are still so strong like the deep roots of the White Oak tree. Even if we fall and cannot seem to muster up the strength to stand it is okay, because the Divine is always there seeing us through, helping to build us up stronger and wiser than before. We have to believe in our capabilities and meet spirit halfway. We have to be willing to see the hidden light in our pain because it's always there. Waiting for us to latch on to it and use it persevere and carry on. Without pain, we wouldn't be able to honor, value, and appreciate pleasure and without pleasure we wouldn't be able to honor, understand and respect our pain.

Future.

Revolution. Reclamation. Reformation. Restoration.

Cosmic Musing #7:
Before the Dawn of Time.

Sometimes I lie awake at night and think about the dawn of time. The time when we telepathically communicated and worshiped the Holy Mother and Father directly. I wonder about all of the ancient technologies, teachings, traditions, and methodologies that were actively in use. Hundreds of thousands of years later and I still feel some of them running through my veins often. Revealing themselves to me in dreams and coming to me in bursts of creativity and inspiration. Asking me to Remember and embrace them deeply. Using me to anchor them in the soils and hearts of today so that we can all reconnect to and remember them wholly once again. Star gazer. Before the dawn of time I've existed. We've existed. But the technologies, teachings, traditions, and methodologies that kept and carried us for millennia have been tainted, distorted, and stolen. Ruthless invaders attempted to wash, erase, and lock it all away forever but what they fail to comprehend is that this type of magic and knowledge can never be destroyed. It is and always will be deeply woven into the blood of the Originals. It was woven into our DNA and our blueprints. Buried deep inside of our bodies for protection and preservation. It's always been etched into the fabric of time and space and no human or being can ever undo that. You can kill the body, traumatize the mind, and destroy the physical information but you cannot destroy the soul and spirit. As long as the Divine is—We are, and there is no technology, or weapon (spiritually or other) that can kill, stop, or silence us or the Divine. It's not on us it is truly in us and many of us are Remembering, Activating, Downloading, and Anchoring for the time of the Sacred Revolution. The one that won't be televised but felt all over the world. It's time for the rise of Nu. It's time for Love to be the way again. It's time the world becomes one for the people again. It's time for the reset. Star gazer. Before the dawn of time. Before the highjacked matrix, the abuse of the divine feminine and the corruption of the divine masculine. When primal was power and the truth was revered and respected. When there was universal and cosmic balance and we all had deep knowing and understanding embedded in our hearts and souls— which allowed us to live and be the salt of the Earth in harmony, unity, and pure eclectic power. Our ancestors knew what was to come and they carefully planned and prepared through ceremonies, sacrifices, and rituals. There was always going to be a destined time in history when all the history and Mysteries they hid in our blood and DNA would rise and awaken. And that time is now. The sphinx and the knowledge hidden within her heart are alive and well, ready to help us remember who we all were and have always been since before the dawn of time so that together we can reclaim what is rightfully ours and rise in togetherness in the name of Love, Freedom, and Liberation of All.

All at Once.

You can look in the mirror and see many different faces.
You see who you used to be and who you've become.
Who you strive to be embodied and the inner child trying to play the
role of a grown-up.
You see the past, present, and future all at once,
reminding us that time is real because our bodies age along it's
demandingness.
Reminding us that time is an illusion because it all unfolds as one.
From the same source,
simultaneous and spontaneous.
The biggest Paradox.
The only thing that has changed is the vessel and the image the mirror
projects.
The heart and the soul remain the same as they did when we were first
born.
But our grievances and pains tell us otherwise as we live and
experience.
They tell us that we have been scarred,
broken into tiny bits and pieces beyond repair and redemption.
That our hearts and souls have been morphed into things
unrecognizable and indigestible.
We play tug of war to see and understand which one holds the truth of
who we really are.
Are we the broken shards of glass riddled with our broken humanity

SOMETIMES I LIE AWAKE AT NIGHT

draped in unforgivable blood,
Or are we who we were when we were first born?
Lambs,
souls full of innocence, wonder, and purity.
Covered in tender kisses— a free spirit absent of bruises, scars, and
all-consuming carnality.
We play tug of war with our minds wondering and fighting for answers
that we feel evade us.
Causing us insanity and pushing us into greater levels of
understanding and awareness.
Are we really losing our minds or are we finally becoming conscious of
it and all that it holds?
Could it be that we are all of the above?
A culmination of our becoming.
While still being a lantern of light,
filled with the essence and substance of the Holy Spirit.
Could it be that we are remembering how to be pure embodiments of
their grace and compassion?
While learning how to harmonize with life in a flow of peace,
tranquility, and acceptance.
Embracing our humanity while still honoring the divinity that lives in
all of us.
It's all so complex and messy.
But alas, this is the beauty and tragedy of the human condition.
Cursed and blessed to be excellent messes of Divine Love and
expression.
Throughout time and space.
Through every fragile breath, we take.
All at once we exist to give life to how Deeply God Loves and wishes
to experience,
The magnitude of their own heart and manifestation.
So all at once, we exist and we thrive in the past, future, and present.

SEYLAH LOVE

Omnipresent— just as our Creator.
Each learning, growing, and evolving with deep intention.
With the purpose of acquiring knowledge and unraveling mysteries
about us, about the One.
The One who is the I am that makes us the We are.
That makes everything and nothing with just a simple heart-filled
intention.
The heart that created all that's in existence.
The one who is responsible for the mountains and the stardust.
For the truth is that we all exist All at Once.
The past version, the present, and the future one.
The broken, mended, and elevated one.
The Lamb, The Lion, and the Dove.
All at once, we breathe all at once
The Earth, our Souls, and the Life force of our Creator.
All at Once we sing, dance, cry, and are haunted.
All at Once we are everything and nothing.
Simple and complex.
Life and Death.
Creation and destruction.
From sun up to sun down,
From the heavens to the deepest oceanic crevices.
Here, there and everywhere that Life can touch.
Because our Creator is and so therefore we are.
Everywhere and everything, separate and apart.
All At Once.
All At Once.

About the Author

Seylah Love (She/They) — I am a Sacred Activist, Multi-Disciplinary Artist, and a full-time Lover, Dreamer, and Being. I love to express myself and the universe within through many creative mediums, but writing creatively and philosophically has always held a very special place in my heart. There have been many times when all I had was my words. They were my life raft, oxygen, medicine, and therapist all in one. They lifted me up when everything around me was pulling me down. They acted as a lighthouse when I was lost and a reviver when my soul lay cold in the dark. It was through writing that the Divine, my ancestors, and Gaia would commune with me. I would use the pen and paper to help me find my way back home and into their arms where peace, unity, and serenity through deep healing awaited me.

I grew up in a small neighborhood called Shrewsbury in New Orleans, Louisiana. I grew up on bounce music, block parties, seafood, and some of the finest Cajun cuisine made with the deepest of love by my grandfather James C. Logwood. I always thank God for allowing me to exist and live at the same time as he did. I don't know who I would've become had I not had his love and influence in my life. He was and always will be, my biggest inspiration, motivator, and reason why. I am who I am because he existed in Love. He is the reason I write with such conviction, fight for truth and justice, and will always strive to be a beacon of love no matter what happens inside or outside of my life. I grew up watching him be such a powerful force of nature, not just within his immediate family but within the community that he served faithfully until his last breath. He was a father, counselor, keeper, safe haven, protector, etc., to many and it was such an honor and a privilege to watch God work through him so purely. He dedicated every day of his life to uplifting and nourishing his community through food, searing presence, and sacred hospitality. Everything I do is in honor of him and every day I strive to continue on his legacy of love and empowered service.

I feel I was very fortunate to grow up in New Orleans because it supplied me with immense richness and depth. The beauty, music, history, and magic that Nola holds and feeds outward never ceases to amaze and inspire me and I am so lucky to have had my soul filled to the brim by such a powerful land. Her strength, resilience, and power run through me and have helped me overcome some of the most challenging times of my life. It was her trees and riverbanks I would sit at as I cried and poured of my grievances and pain. It was her arms I ran into to find solace and comfort in the times it felt like the world was constantly caving in under my feet. It was the whispers of my ancestors through the trees and their blood deep in her roots that helped me find my way back home to the Divine and myself. The love, guidance, and support of my ancestors helped me discover and reconnect to the truth, light, beauty, love, and power that lies within me. They believed in me and fought with me when no one else would and they continue to do so every step of the way. When I write they get a chance to tell their stories too. They get a chance to let their voices and souls be heard, witnessed, and felt. They get to share their powerful testimonies of resolve, faith, and resilience for all to see and feel empowered by. I don't write just for me but for Us. For the collective healing and empowerment of our lineage and blood. This is for the liberation of our unified soul and the illumination of all the voices that were forcibly silenced, disregarded, and/or forgotten. Every time I write a chain is broken. An ancestor is engulfed in light and a wound is healed by the balm that is truth and righteousness. This is our rebellion and revolution. So yes I am a full-time fighter because I will never stop using my words and my voice to fight for the healing, empowerment, and liberation of my blood, but also for the healing, empowerment, and liberation of all those oppressed, chained, and suffering at the hands of wickedness no matter the shape, form or context. I will continue to write to inform and bring awareness to the overlooked, silenced, and neglected because every heartbeat matters and has the right to be honored and treated with dignity, respect, and deep care. Every heartbeat has the right to true freedom, a full life, and Soulful liberation.

I will keep fighting but I will also keep loving as deeply and unconditionally as I possibly can. To me, being a sacred activist means being a warrior for love, truth, and justice. Not just speaking about it but BEING about it. Being a pure vessel for the Divine to work through as you vow to guard, protect, and honor the wonder, beauty, divinity/mystery, and innocence in all things. It means holding sacred space and advocating for all living things so that they may be heard, witnessed, and embraced respectfully in all of their being.

As a divine physician and universal sage, I utilize the higher knowledge and wisdom I have obtained through my personal experiences and academic studies to help guide, teach, and support others as they traverse along their own unique and sacred paths of spiritual and personal growth, healing, development, and expansion. When I began my spiritual journey and even as I simply journeyed through life, I did not have the proper support or guidance I needed to be able to travel or learn as safely as I could have. In turn, I found myself in a lot of harmful, traumatic, and sometimes dangerous situations and experiences that I could have avoided, had I had the proper direction and support and so a huge part of my mission is to provide that support, guidance, and safe space to others. To help them learn through sharing my trials, tribulations, and testimonies. I want to help others become the highest, most embodied versions of themselves so that they can tap into their fullest potential and embrace and live in their purpose as powerfully and potently as they can. I wish to do this with my writings, through music and community building and nourishment. I'm very grateful and excited to be able to share more of myself, love, and energy here with you all. Thank you all from the bottom of my heart for reading and holding space for these words. I pray these words inspire you, Awaken you, and hold you down while lifting you up just as they do for me. Thank you.

Don't miss out!

Visit the website below and you can sign up to receive emails whenever Seylah Love publishes a new book. There's no charge and no obligation.

https://books2read.com/r/B-A-YKKMC-QZPAF

* 9 7 9 8 2 2 7 5 0 8 1 9 5 *